Beckett Great Sports Heroes

# Troy Aikman

By the staff of Beckett Publications

House of Collectibles • New York

RR TH BP RG GH NL

**H** This is a registered trademark of Random House, Inc.

Published by: House of Collectibles
201 East 50th Street
New York, NY 10022

Distributed by Ballantine Books, a division of Random House, Inc., New York,
and simultaneously in Canada by Random House of Canada Limited, Toronto.

Manufactured in the United States of America
ISBN: 0-676-60035-2

Cover design by Michaelis & Carpelis Design Associates, Inc.

Cover photo by Bob Rosato
Back cover photos by (left to right) Mitchell B. Reibel; Allen Kee

First Edition: July 1996

10    9    8    7    6    5    4    3    2    1

The Publisher would like to thank Dr. James Beckett
and the staff of Beckett Publications for providing the editorial and photo content of this book.

Managing Editor Gary Santaniello and Art Director Lisa McQuilkin Monaghan had the able editorial, design and production assistance of
Barbara Barry, Rob Barry, Therese Bellar, Amy Brougher, Emily Camp, Theo Chen, Belinda Cross, Randy Cummings, Marlon DePaula,
Gail Docekal, Eric Evans, Barbara Faraldo, Kim Ford, Mary Gonzalez-Davis, Tracy Hackler, Pepper Hastings, Paul Kerutis, Rudy J. Klancnik, Benedito Leme,
Sara Leeman, Lori Lindsey, Teri McGahey, Sara Maneval, Louis Marroquin, Mike McAllister, Daniel Moscoso Jr., Randy Mosty, Lisa O'Neill, Mike Pagel,
Mike Payne, Tim Polzer, Reed Poole, Will Pry, Fred Reed III, Tina Riojas, Susan Sainz, Judi Smalling, Jeff Stanton, Doug Williams, Steve Wilson and Mark Zeske.


Additionally, the Publisher would like to acknowledge the entire staff of Beckett Publications, which was instrumental in the completion of this book: Dana Alecknavage,
Jeff Amano, Jeff Anthony, Kelly Atkins, Claire Backus, Kaye Ball, Airey Baringer, Randy Barning, Eric Best, Julie Binion, Louise Bird, Cathryn Black, Pat Blandford, Marco Brizuela,
Bob Brown, Chris Calandro, Randall Calvert, Mary Campana, Susan Catka, Jud Chappell, Albert Chavez, Dawn Ciaccio, Marty Click, Cindy Cockroft, Laura Corley, Andres Costilla,
Lauren Drewes, Ben Ecklar, Craig Ferris, Gean Paul Figari, Jeany Finch, Joe Galindo, Gayle Gasperin, Stephen Genusa, Loretta Gibbs, Marcelo Gomes de Souza,
Rosanna Gonzalez-Olaechea, Duane Green, Jeff Greer, Mary Gregory, Robert Gregory, Jenifer Grellhesl, Julie Grove, Patti Harris, Leslie Harris, Mark Harwell,
Beth Harwell, Joanna Hayden, Chris Hellem, Dan Hitt, Mike Jaspersen, Jay Johnson, Steven Judd, Eddie Kelly, Wendy Kizer, Rich Klein, Brian Kosley, Tom Layberger,
Jane Ann Layton, Stanley Lira, Kirk Lockhart, Lisa Lujan, John Marshall, Omar Mediano, Beverly Mills, Sherry Monday, Rob Moore, Mila Morante, Mike Moss, Allan Muir,
Shawn Murphy, Hugh Murphy, Mike Obert, Stacy Olivieri, Wendy Pallugna, Laura Patterson, Gabriel Rangel, Bob Richardson, Grant Sandground, David Schneider, Brett Setter,
Elaine Simmons, Dave Sliepka, Sheri Smith, Rob Springs, Phaedra Strecher, Margaret Steele, Marcia Stoesz, Doree Tate, Jim Tereschuk and Carol Weaver.

Foreword

# Destiny's Darling

**A seemingly inconsequential pro football game set in motion Troy Aikman's ascent to greatness and stardom**

On the final weekend of the 1988 season, Green Bay quarterback Don Majkowski threw two touchdown passes to rally the Packers past the Cardinals, 26-17. That result set in motion a chain of events for which the Dallas Cowboys are eternally grateful and which likely changed the course of NFL history.

Majkowski's magic provided the Packers with their fourth win of the season. The Cowboys, who had lost to Philadelphia that same afternoon, stood alone with the worst record in the league at 3-13.

Two weeks later, the city of Dallas watched as the UCLA's Bruins, led by All-America quarterback Troy Aikman, beat Arkansas in the 1989 Cotton Bowl. It would be Aikman's final collegiate game but his first in the city that soon would embrace him as a hero.

The Cowboys, with the first overall pick in April's draft, chose Aikman. Seven years and three Super Bowl championships later, Aikman is regarded by many as the NFL's top quarterback on the NFL's greatest team. He also may be the most popular person — in or out of sports — in the Dallas-Fort Worth Metroplex.

Just 29 years old, Aikman appears destined for additional glory. Not for what he may accomplish in the future, though, but for what he already has accomplished, we salute the Cowboys' great No. 8 — Troy Aikman.

**Troy's success as a Dallas Cowboy has given him plenty of reasons to smile.**

*Mike Pagel*
Mike Pagel
Assistant Editor

# CONTENTS

While restoring pride and luster to the city of Dallas and its football franchise, Troy Aikman not only established himself as one of the NFL's fiercest competitors, but he also became one of America's most popular quarterbacks

star

By Ken Sins

t roy Aikman faced the challenge of performing for two football teams during the 1989 Cotton Bowl game in Dallas.

As the senior star quarterback prepared to lead his UCLA Bruins against the Arkansas Razorbacks, he couldn't help being distracted by thoughts of his professional career, which was just a few months away.

The Dallas Cowboys owned the first overall pick in the upcoming NFL draft, and they already had announced their intentions of grabbing Aikman. The Cowboys had finished the season with a league-worst 3-13 record, and they were desperately in need of a savior to return the franchise to past glories. Aikman would be the first piece to the rebuilding puzzle.

The pressure became overwhelming for a country boy who was far more comfortable riding the fenceline in his hometown of Henryetta, Okla., than he was in glitzy Los Angeles or Dallas.

But Aikman felt it necessary to show the folks in his future home that he was ready for prime time, while simultaneously rewarding Bruins fans for their loyalty with a smashing victory over Arkansas.

"That whole period was really, really strange," Aikman says, smiling and shaking his head at the memory. "If I ever write a book, that part will be really interesting. It was fun, but it was also nerve-racking. I wanted to do well in the Cotton Bowl, I guess because I felt deep down that I would be playing here. It was important for me to come out and play well and at least give the people here some kind of hope that I'd be a good player for the city."

All parties agreed that once the game was over, Troy Aikman's life

would take a radical turn.

Aikman responded to the enormous expectations with a poised, efficient show that provided Cowboys fans with a glimpse of a glorious future. He was voted the game's offensive MVP, completing 19-of-27 passes for 172 yards in a 17-3 victory over the Southwest Conference champs. *(For more on the '89 Cotton Bowl game, see page 75.)*

He's been under the gun, and

**Through his days at UCLA, Troy Aikman dreamed of one day shining in the NFL.**

under a microscope ever since. And he's delivered a series of high-profile big-game performances that make him a cinch Hall of Famer.

Aikman has engineered the Cowboys' unprecedented three Super Bowl titles in four seasons, playing flawlessly when it has mattered most. In the

Cowboys' latest triumph in Super Bowl XXX, Aikman was on pace to win the Most Valuable Player Award before cornerback Larry Brown's late interception sealed the 27-17 victory over the Pittsburgh Steelers and swayed MVP voters.

His most recent Super Bowl numbers once again were solid: 15 completions in 23 attempts for 209 yards and one touchdown. As important as what Aikman did on that cool evening in the Arizona desert is what he didn't do. He played the entire game without throwing an interception. Almost without fail, every split-second decision he made was the proper one. At one point, he completed 10 consecutive passes, falling three short of Joe Montana's Super Bowl record.

Aikman now ranks third on the NFL's all-time list for Super Bowl victories by a quarterback, trailing just Montana and Terry Bradshaw, both of whom finished their careers at 4-0.

Need more convincing that Aikman has the right stuff when games mean the most? His postseason record dating back to the 1992 season now stands at 10-1. His playoff completion percentage is 68, best of all-time, and his quarterback rating over that span rates at 104.3, second only to Bart Starr's 104.8 rating. If not for a first-quarter interception in the divisional playoff win over Philadelphia last season, Aikman would have duplicated his run of no interceptions in the 1992 playoffs.

"I like everything that the playoffs represent," Aikman says. "I like the finality of it: Winner takes all, loser goes home. I enjoy the sense of urgency that comes with that."

As Aikman enters his eighth season, he already has stepped over the threshold and into NFL history. You won't hear Aikman spouting those gaudy statistics, however. In Aikman's estimation, the true measure of a quarterback is what his team accomplishes.

"After having done this three times in four years, certainly this team has made a place in history," Aikman says. "It's something that hasn't been done before and that is very rewarding to all of us."

although Aikman endured the typical trials a quarterback must face early in his NFL career, it was clear from his first training camp he was something special. Within four years, Aikman was a Super Bowl MVP, an All-Pro hailed as the most complete quarterback in the league and the NFL's highest-paid player.

All three Super Bowl rides have presented challenges for Aikman.

# head of the class

With Aikman in charge, the Cowboys have enjoyed prolific playoff success

If postseason performances are the best criteria to grade the success of an NFL quarterback, then Troy Aikman scores an A+.

Aikman's mastery of pressure-packed playoff situations sparked the Dallas Cowboys to three Super Bowl wins in four seasons. And his record of 10-1 as a starter in playoff games rates among the best ever.

Great quarterbacks such as Montana, Bradshaw and Theismann boast more playoff wins, but it's Aikman's winning percentage and Super Bowl success that stands out.

Aikman's playoff experiences began in a backup role following a late-season knee injury in 1991. Dallas won a Wild Card playoff game in Chicago with Steve Beuerlein as the team's quarterback. The following week Aikman came off the bench to throw 11 completions in 16 attempts for 114 yards in a loss to Detroit.

Aikman, however, stayed healthy enough the next four seasons to start all of the Cowboys playoff games. He quickly rose to the top of the class.

Aikman capped off the 1992 postseason — his best ever — by claiming the Super Bowl XXVII MVP Award. In the three Cowboys playoff victories, Aikman completed 61 of 89 passes for 795 yards, eight touch-

**The following is Aikman's career playoff statistical chart:**

| Year | Record | Att. | Comp. | Yds. | Pct. | TD | Int. | Rating |
|------|--------|------|-------|------|------|----|----|--------|
| 1991 | 0-0 | 16 | 11 | 114 | 68.8 | 0 | 1 | 63.0 |
| 1992 | 3-0 | 89 | 61 | 795 | 68.5 | 8 | 0 | 126.4 |
| 1993 | 3-0 | 82 | 61 | 686 | 74.4 | 5 | 3 | 104.0 |
| 1994 | 1-1 | 83 | 53 | 717 | 63.9 | 4 | 4 | 87.3 |
| 1995 | 3-0 | 80 | 53 | 717 | 66.3 | 4 | 1 | 106.1 |
| Totals | 10-1 | 350 | 239 | 3,029 | 68.3 | 21 | 9 | 104.6 |

"Each one has been a little different," he says. "The first one was by far the most fun. The second one was rewarding for all of us because we did it back-to-back and had to overcome a lot of adversity. We had to stay focused to do it twice in a row.

"This year we overcame a great deal as well. All along I've felt that this team overcame more than the other two Super Bowl teams had. It's a very rewarding feeling. It's a sense of relief for all of us."

Aikman also knows that the pressure to repeat began as soon as the confetti from the latest victory parade was being swept up.

"It's a vicious cycle," he says.

As the Cowboys enter the 1996 NFL season, many prognosticators rank Dallas as a heavy favorite to represent the NFC in Super Bowl XXXI in New Orleans. Anything short of another championship game appearance for Dallas probably will be considered a disappointing season. The cycle continues.

downs and no interceptions.

Aikman helped the Cowboys successfully defend their NFL title the following season by completing nearly 75 percent of his passes in victories over Green Bay, San Francisco and Buffalo.

In the 1994 NFC Championship Game, the San Francisco 49ers handed Aikman his lone playoff loss as a starter, 38-28.

One year later, Aikman and the Cowboys returned to the top with another Super Bowl victory, this time at the hands of the Pittsburgh Steelers.

At age 29, Aikman already stands as a legend among playoff heroes. And it's quite possible that in future seasons he and the Cowboys will continue taking the rest of the league to school.

— *Mike Pagel*

Since his arrival into the league, Aikman has been the Cowboys' unquestioned leader. NFL scouts didn't express any doubt regarding Aikman's physical gifts. When the Cowboys exercised the no-brain option of making him the first overall selection in that draft, they realized he had it all: the rifle arm, the soft touch on finesse passes and the 6-4, 228-pound package that allowed him to hang in the pocket and absorb punishment through the early years.

But the Cowboys found that there was more to Aikman than just his physical attributes. Aikman has mastered the mental game. He demands control in the huddle. He consistently makes intelligent decisions with the game on the line. And he makes demands of teammates that usually are met.

"He's got the stare," Cowboys

**Whether he's suiting up for real or participating in an NFL Quarterback Challenge, Aikman always plays the role of a cool competitor.**

scouting director Larry Lacewell says.

In other words, Aikman commands respect. His eyes tell both teammates and opponents that the job will get done, that heroic deeds are about to be accomplished.

The 29-year-old Aikman is at the top of his profession as the league's finest all-around quarterback. He earned his fifth consecutive Pro Bowl selection to tie Roger Staubach for the most in a row by a Cowboys QB. He's in the midst of an eight-year, $50 million contract and is hungry to join Montana and Bradshaw with their collections of four Super Bowl rings.

"I think when you talk about Troy Aikman, you're talking about a real classy individual," running back Emmitt Smith says. "He keeps fighting back. That's the type of person he is. He's a true champion."

Indeed, the essence of Aikman is his fiercely competitive nature. He's a perfectionist who tolerates nothing less than the best effort from teammates.

**t**roy Kenneth Aikman is handsome and intelligent. He's one of the best-known athletes on the planet, but he is basically an uncomplicated man, a bachelor who avoids the allure of the Dallas night life that has swallowed so many of his predecessors and contemporaries. A big night out for Aikman is a few games of pool and a Country and Western show with a few college pals.

Although Aikman once was named one of America's 50 Most Beautiful People by *People* magazine, flaunting his celebrity isn't Aikman's style. Some have speculated that Aikman is so consumed by the game and winning that he will postpone marriage until his football days are over.

To those who expect a more high-profile social and commercial presence from Aikman, he offers no apologies.

"I am what I am," he says. "People who see me are either turned on by that or they're not. I can't be all things to all people."

He maintains his competitive edge in part by remembering his roots. Through his first two seasons, defeats piled on his shoulders like boulders. He

**On game day, Troy Aikman typically displays a stern look of concentration and intensity.**

went 0-11 as a rookie starter and 7-8 his second season. Injuries forced him to miss 10 games during his first three seasons.

"I haven't forgotten that and I don't want to," Aikman says. "I think having gone through that in '89, as painful as that was, it has really helped me. Each year it makes me realize how fragile success is.

"It's very hard to win in this league," Aikman admits. "I was able to learn that my first year here. I've continued to remember that. With each game, with each season that goes by, it

# n o   f i f t h   w h e e l

**Much to the delight of racer Sterling Marlin, Troy Aikman radiates a winning fever whether he's on the football field or on pit row**

NIGEL KINRADE

When it comes to winning, Troy Aikman isn't limited to just football.

In 1994, less than a month after leading the Cowboys to their second consecutive Super Bowl victory, Aikman served as the starter for the Daytona 500 stock car race. He watched the season-opening event, considered NASCAR's "Super Bowl," as an honorary pit crew member for veteran driver Sterling Marlin.

Aikman even wore one of the yellow uniform shirts of Marlin's team, which is sponsored by Kodak. The quarterback's magic touch rubbed off as Marlin captured his first Winston Cup victory in 280 career starts.

Aikman celebrated the win in victory lane with the Kodak team and even stayed with Marlin through his post-

**If a victory lane existed in football, Aikman would be a frequent visitor.**

race interviews. But the quarterback refused to give autographs or give his own extensive interviews, saying that he didn't want to spoil Marlin's big moment.

Marlin, a native of Tennessee, first met Aikman through mutual friends in country music. The two have developed a solid friendship and often attend the other's events to provide support.

Marlin has been Aikman's guest at several Cowboys playoff games, all of which Dallas has won. Marlin's NASCAR career has taken off since Aikman's visit to victory lane. He became just the third driver to win two consecutive Daytona 500s when he repeated his 1994 victory the next year. Marlin finished third in the season points standings and won three races in 1995, both career highs.
— *Mark Zeske*

ALLEN KEE / BRSP

# beckett remembers

No one personifies the Dallas Cowboys as much as its on-field general, Troy Aikman. From his 1-15 NFL debut in 1989 to his third Super Bowl victory just last January, Aikman has endured the jeers and enjoyed the cheers from fans across the country.

*Beckett Football Card Monthly* recognized Aikman as a winner early in his career and featured him on his first BFCM cover at the beginning of his third season (October, 1991 issue #19).

In just his fourth season on the pro circuit, Aikman led the Cowboys to their first Super Bowl victory in 15 years and thus landed his second *BFCM* cover with the April 1993 issue (#37). Aikman's envious performance during Super Bowl XXVII allowed him to join Jim Plunkett and Terry Bradshaw as the only quarterbacks drafted first overall to be named Super Bowl MVP.

With a tough act to follow the next season, Aikman responded by quarterbacking the Cowboys to their second consecutive Super Bowl victory. He also ventured his way onto his third *BFCM* cover (January 1994, issue #46).

Four months later, *BFCM* celebrated its 50th issue with a cover featuring some of the most notable faces in NFL history. Fittingly, Aikman takes his place beside Joe Namath, Terry Bradshaw and Joe Montana in Gerald Tysver, Jr.'s artistic rendition of *Great Quarterbacks*.

Troy also graced the cover of *BFCM's* February 1995 issue (#59) after the Cowboys endured perhaps their most disappointing season in the past five years; they failed to make it to the Super Bowl. Not one to be held back though, Aikman rallied his troops and led them to victory in Super Bowl XXX, their third world championship in just four years.

With more fantastic moments on the horizon for Troy Aikman, you can bet that Beckett Publications will be there to highlight those good times. And unless you're an NFL defensive coordinator, you'll enjoy celebrating Troy's continued success as much as you have in the past.

— *Doug Williams*

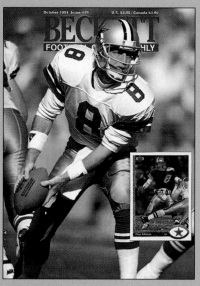

**BFCM #19**

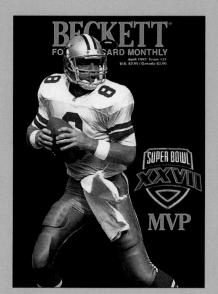

**BFCM #37**

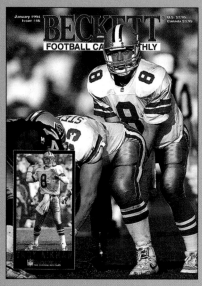

**BFCM #46**

**BFCM #50**

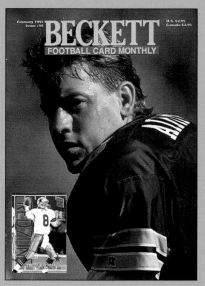

**BFCM #59**

keeps me focused and keeps me continually wanting to go out and work and do the things necessary to give me a chance to be successful."

Don't get the wrong idea. Nobody's

**Even for the reigning champion, earning a trip back to the Super Bowl remains Aikman's No. 1 priority.**

suggesting that Aikman's been a one-man band. Behind Aikman is Smith, a four-time rushing champion who's already considered to be one of the best runners in NFL history. Smith's game-breaking threat creates openings in the passing game for Aikman and a talented group of receivers led by All-Pro Michael Irvin. Protecting Aikman is the league's biggest, toughest offensive

line. Fullback Daryl Johnston has developed into an excellent blocker and safety-valve receiver. Without a doubt, the key to Aikman's success is Dallas' offensive balance.

But other quarterbacks surrounded by talent have squandered Super Bowl opportunities; Aikman has cashed in three, including an MVP performance in Super Bowl XXVII.

Early in his career, Aikman wore the tag of an injury-prone player. A few misguided fans were actually lobbying for Aikman's backup at the time, Steve Walsh, to take over the starting position.

Aikman has sustained a broken finger on his throwing hand, as well as back, elbow and knee problems. Last season brought knee, back, calf and elbow ailments. In 1995, he started all 16 games in the regular season for the first time since 1992, and was healthy throughout the playoffs. Successful surgery removed bone chips from his right elbow during the off-season, and Aikman says he'll be ready for 1996 training camp.

"I've taken my share of hits and had my share of injuries," Aikman says. "I know that last season, every day I got up I felt pain in my knees and lower back. I've never wanted to be one of those guys who gets out of bed moaning and groaning about the pain you endure."

Every hit he takes pushes him closer to retirement, although he says there's still enough tread on his tires for a couple more Super Bowl runs.

A couple more?

"I'd like to win five because that's something no one else has done," Aikman says.

Don't bet against him. As a big-game quarterback, he's capable of anything. •

*Ken Sins is a freelance writer based in Dallas.*

LOUIS DeLUCA

# SUPER!

Troy Aikman's status as a modern-day legend has grown stronger based on his three Super Bowl performances

AL BELLO / ALLSPORT USA

# A New Dynasty Dawns

Just three seasons after suffering through a 1-15 season, Aikman found himself on top of the NFL world as Super Bowl MVP

**By Vic Carucci**

Ten minutes into Super Bowl XXVII, Troy Aikman had completed three of six passes for a meager 17 yards, and his Dallas Cowboys trailed the Buffalo Bills, 7-0.

Aikman looked jittery. The Cowboys were out of sync on offense. And the Bills — thanks to a Thurman Thomas touchdown set up by a blocked punt by Steve Tasker — appeared primed to snap their two-game Super Bowl losing streak.

Then reality hit Buffalo harder than an Aikman bullet pass between the eyes.

Dallas safety James Washington intercepted a Jim Kelly pass and returned it to the Bills' 47. Six plays later, Aikman zipped a game-tying 23-yard touchdown strike over the middle to tight end Jay Novacek.

Gone were Aikman's Super Bowl butterflies . . . and Buffalo's chances to win the game.

Aikman went on to throw two touchdown passes to Michael Irvin 32 seconds apart late in the second quarter. Then, a game-breaking 45-yard scoring bomb to Alvin Harper with 10:04 left in the game secured his status as the Most Valuable Player in Dallas' 52-17 Rose Bowl romp.

"We started off pretty shaky," says Aikman, who finished 22-of-30 for 273 yards and the four TDs. "We had problems getting lined up and getting the right plays and running them right. I was a little nervous, every player was a little nervous.

"But once we settled down, it became a normal game."

Of course, "normal" for Aikman translated into trouble for the opposition in 1992. He had set career highs for completions (302), passing yards (3,445) and touchdowns (23) in leading Dallas to a 13-3 regular-season record.

Somehow, the fourth-year veteran elevated his already superb game to a new dimension in the postseason. In playoff victories over Philadelphia and San Francisco, Aikman completed 66.1 percent of his passes for 522 yards, four TDs and no interceptions.

As helpless as the Eagles and 49ers were against Aikman, they weren't as incompetent as the Bills. At the start, Buffalo concentrated on stopping Dallas' two wideouts, Irvin and Harper. No problem. Aikman just utilized Novacek on crossing routes over the middle. He completed five passes to Novacek in the first half, and as soon as the Bills changed their coverage, Aikman adjusted again.

"Troy was definitely in a zone," running back Emmitt Smith says. "Once he had time, he picked out his receivers accordingly and got the ball to them and let them be runners after that."

Leading just 14-10 with two minutes left in the first half, Aikman recognized single coverage on Irvin and hit him for a 19-yard touchdown. Thomas fumbled on the ensuing offensive play — one of a Super Bowl-record nine Buffalo turnovers — and Aikman quickly went to work, burning another man-to-man coverage with an 18-yard TD pass to Irvin for a 28-10 halftime lead.

"Troy said we have to be patient outside and keep going inside to Jay until they came out of it," Irvin recalls. "We had one-on-one outside [on his two scores], and when we have that, we take advantage of it. Troy did a great job seeing it and taking advantage of it."

The Super Bowl victory was the first by a Dallas team since 1977, when Roger Staubach led the Cowboys to a 27-10 win over Denver in Super Bowl XII.

Based on Aikman's postseason performance in '92, most prognosticators expected him to lead the Cowboys to many more Super Bowl games in his career — beginning with a rematch in one year against a Buffalo team starving for a title.  •

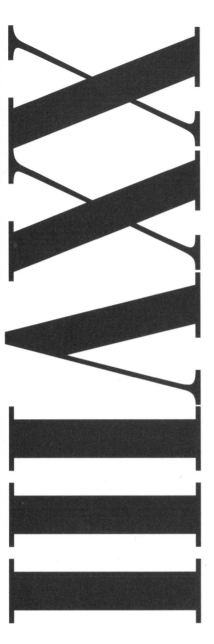

# Encore

**Back on the NFL's grandest stage, Aikman stepped forth with another game-winning performance**

**By Vic Carucci**

Troy Aikman felt more like sighing than celebrating after the Dallas Cowboys' 30-13 victory over the Buffalo Bills in Super Bowl XXVIII.

"Since [the previous] Super Bowl ended, we've had to deal with the pressure about going back and repeating and winning it all again," says Aikman, who became just the fifth quarterback in NFL history to lead his team to back-to-back Super Bowl triumphs. "It's taken its toll. This year wasn't as much fun. It was more of a struggle.

"But it was every bit as satisfying."

The final score made the game seem far easier than it actually was for the Cowboys — and for Aikman in particular. Through the first half in the Georgia Dome, it appeared as if the Bills might, once and for all, end their three-game Super Bowl hex.

Dallas took a 6-3 lead in the first quarter on a pair of Eddie Murray field goals. But after Murray's second kick, the Bills answered with a 17-play, 80-yard march capped by Thurman Thomas' 4-yard touchdown run.

Then, with 1:03 left in the first half, Nate Odomes intercepted an Aikman pass intended for receiver Alvin Harper and returned it 41 yards to the Dallas 47. Kelly maneuvered the Bills into position for Steve Christie's 28-yard field goal at the gun, giving the Bills a 13-6 halftime edge.

"The interception was all my fault," Harper says. "I should have broken in instead of going out."

Aikman, despite lingering effects from a concussion in the NFC Championship Game just a week earlier, was as consistent in the first half as he had been all season. He completed an efficient 12 of 16 passes, but produced just 121 yards and no touchdowns. The Cowboys also had posted just 50 yards rushing and 10 first downs.

Coming back out onto the field for the second half, Aikman knew that Emmitt Smith would be the key to winning the game.

Almost instantly, the Dallas defense provided Aikman and Smith an opportunity to install their ball-control offense.

On the third play of the third quarter, Cowboys defensive tackle Leon Lett forced a Thomas fumble. Safety James Washington scooped it up and returned it 46 yards for a touchdown, tying the game and irrevocably swinging the momentum in Dallas' favor.

After a three-and-out Bills series, the Cowboys went for the jugular. Aikman handed the ball to Smith seven times on an eight-play, 64-yard drive that ended with Smith scoring on a 15-yard run.

"We were able to get some big gains so we stuck with it throughout that drive," Aikman says. "And once we got that going, our big linemen up front started to wear Buffalo down."

Aikman threw just 11 passes in the second half as MVP Smith piled up 91 yards on the ground and Dallas controlled the ball for nearly 17 minutes.

Dallas combination of Smith and Aikman was too much for the Bills defense to handle. Smith finished the game with 132 yards on 30 carries, while Aikman completed a tidy 19 of 27 passes for 207 yards.

Meanwhile, the Bills suffered an incomprehensible fourth straight Super Bowl loss, a streak that weighs heaviest on quarterback Jim Kelly. Aikman has genuine sympathy for his Buffalo counterpart.

"Jim is a good friend of mine," he says. "I wish that every football player could walk away from the game with a championship ring because it's a special deal. And I hope that Jim gets one." •

*Vic Carucci covered Super Bowl XXVII and XXVIII for the* Buffalo News.

## Like a Rock

**Behind Stonewall Aikman's steady charge, Dallas captured its third Super Bowl title in four years**

**By Gerry Dulac**

Carnell Lake knows a smile when he doesn't see one. And as the Steelers Pro Bowl safety glances across the line of scrimmage, he rarely sees one on the face of Troy Aikman.

Lake never saw it when the two were teammates at UCLA, and he never saw it during Super Bowl XXX.

"He doesn't smile a lot," Lake says. "He just gets right back in the pocket and he doesn't worry about the pressure."

The one emotion Aikman did display when Super Bowl XXX came to a dramatic close was relief — relief that a season in which the Cowboys were under so much self-imposed pressure had come to an end, thankfully, with a 27-17 victory against the Steelers on a warm Sunday night in Tempe, Ariz. Relief also in that Aikman again survived an overwhelming amount of pressure to lead Dallas to an unprecedented third Super Bowl championship in four years.

"I have never been so happy for a season to be over," Aikman admitted afterward.

For Aikman, though, the triumph put him on track to join Terry Bradshaw and Joe Montana as quarterbacks with perfect 4-0 records in Super Bowl play. "It's his time of the year," wide receiver Michael Irvin says.

The Steelers' pregame strategy focused on stopping Emmitt Smith, the NFL's leading rusher. They had fretted over the size of the Cowboys' mammoth offensive line and its power blocking techniques.

But the Steelers did stop Smith, holding him to just 49 yards on 18 carries, and that after a 23-yard run on the game's third play. He managed just 9 yards on seven carries in the second half.

Stopping Aikman too, however, might have been too much to ask of the Steelers' defense.

Aikman is like a great baseball pitcher. If you don't rattle him early, you're in for a long night. And, with the exception of two incompletions on the first series, the Steelers didn't blast out of the gate and chase Aikman back to Dallas.

Oh, Aikman started slowly, completing only one of his first three passes, but the one was a 20-yarder to Irvin that moved the ball to the Cowboys' 49 and set up Chris Boniol's 42-yard field goal.

From there, Aikman did not miss another pass on the next two series. Despite his slow start, Aikman still posted his usual consistent game — 15 of 23 for 209 yards, one touchdown and no interceptions.

Aikman deftly spread the Steelers' defense with passes to his wide receivers. Then he would cross up outside linebackers Kevin Greene and Greg Lloyd by throwing underneath to tight end Jay Novacek. This strategy worked to perfection when Aikman connected on a 47-yard pass to cornerback-turned-receiver Deion Sanders. Moments later, Aikman hit Novacek for a 3-yard touchdown pass, and before the Steelers could blink, the deficit was 10-0.

Aikman's assault on the Pittsburgh defense continued as he set up a field goal on Dallas' next possession with a 19-yard completion to Novacek.

The Steelers tried, but could not recover from what eventually became a 20-7 Dallas lead.

"Every time he throws the ball it's always a perfect throw," says Novacek, who finished with five catches for 50 yards. "That's hard to get from any other quarterback."

Aikman, with or without a smile, is not just any other quarterback.　　•

*Gerry Dulac covered Super Bowl XXX for the* Pittsburgh Post-Gazette.

# 3OFA

Troy Aikman may have established
Bowl titles, but how does he stack

MEREDITH

By Frank Luksa

himself as one for the ages by winning three Super
up to two other legendary Cowboys quarterbacks?

KIND

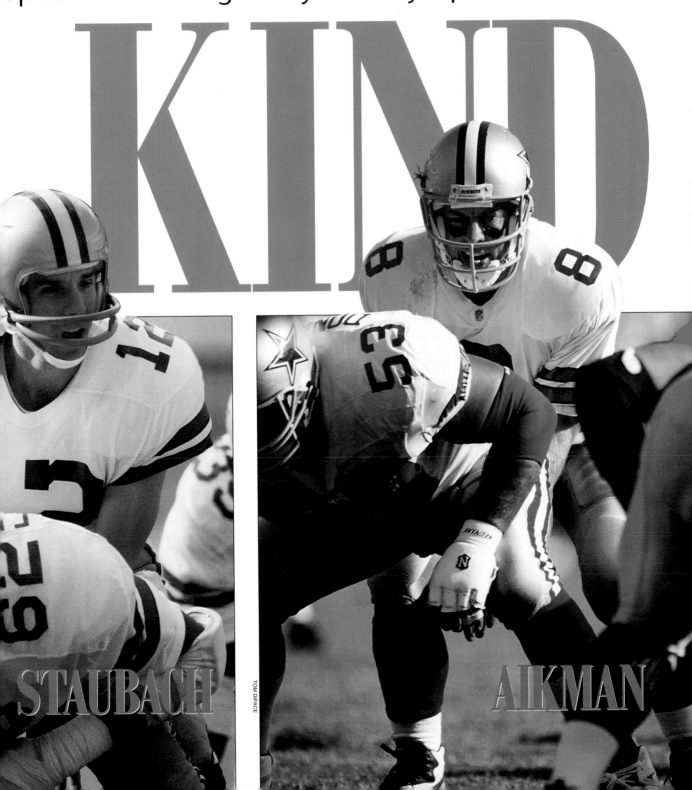

STAUBACH

TOM DiPACE

AIKMAN

The Dallas Cowboys have produced three exceptional quarterbacks through their eventful 26-year history: Don Meredith, Roger Staubach and Troy Aikman. Each proved himself a winner to varying degree and left historians an issue to ponder:

Was one of them better than the other two?

Meredith helped the Cowboys post their first winning season, playoff victory and division title. Staubach led the franchise to its first two Super Bowl crowns. And Aikman became the first quarterback in NFL history to guide a team to three Super Bowl titles within a span of four years.

Each moved more than the proverbial grain of sand during his career. All three left footprints as monuments to success. But whose are the deepest?

The variance between these quarterbacks as pure passers, team leaders, winners of championships and personalities often rises as the subject of intense debate. So it shall be as Meredith, Staubach and Aikman are compared and contrasted on those terms.

Three factors complicate the task. First, the quarterbacks were alike to the point of being inseparable in terms of physical courage. But because of rules changes, the game each played was different and thus tilted individual statistics for better or worse. And finally, none knew a supporting cast of equal strength or became a starter at the same stage of his career.

Meredith was the most-often and most-seriously hurt. His worst injury was a punctured lung that sent him to the hospital. Staubach once played the second half with fractured ribs that disabled him the next week. Aikman has always returned to the lineup sooner than expected from an injury. All exhibited an iron will to play through pain and all rank equal on a scale of physical toughness.

Career numbers alone place Meredith as the third-best passer. His 50.7 completion percentage trails Staubach (57.0) and Aikman (62.8). His

MEREDITH

74.7 rating is far below the 83.5 shared by Staubach and Aikman.

Passing during Meredith's 1960-68 era was much more difficult than it is today. Rules favored defenses. Pass rushers used head slaps against linemen required to fix hands to their chests. Defensive backs could physically engage receivers until the ball was in the air.

A poor offensive line as late as 1964 further increased Meredith's handicap. During that 14-game season, he suffered an astonishing 58 sacks. Yet, he still accomplished the top-three passing games in Cowboys history with efforts of 460, 406 and 394 yards. Meredith also accounted for the Cowboys' longest ever pass completion of 95 yards, to Bob Hayes.

Of the three, Meredith had the most individual flair and personal magnetism. Opponents even remarked of a saucy style that drew others to him.

"He has this charisma about him," says former Los Angeles Rams great Merlin Olsen. "He's like Bobby Layne, a great player and leader, and an exciting person just to be around. Meredith is to me what I want and expect an NFL quarterback to be."

But Meredith's fate is to be remembered for losing NFL title games to Green Bay in 1966 and '67. For forfeiting the NFC passing title in '68 to Earl Morrall with a careless 1-for-9 show in the regular season finale. For being booed like no other as the focal point of fan frustration. And perhaps as a composite result, for retiring prematurely at age 31.

He left the NFL as a three-time Pro Bowler, with a 2-4 playoff record and no All-Pro mention or passing titles. Some suggested his early departure was hastened by a free-spirit persona that never adapted to coach Tom Landry's rigid system.

**D**iscipline came naturally to Staubach, the 1963 Heisman Trophy winner at Navy, who joined the Cowboys after a four-year hitch in the service.

Winning also came naturally to Staubach. The Cowboys won at a .726 clip (85-29) under him during regular season play, never posted a losing record and never were shut

AIKMAN

ALLEN KEE / BRSP

# STAUBACH

out during his tenure (1969-79).

Staubach's specialty was winning from behind. He led 23 comeback victories in the fourth quarter or in overtime. That remarkable stat magnified his value to the Cowboys beyond the measure of Meredith or Aikman.

"Roger is the difference in that team and he would be the same wherever he was," says former Houston Oilers coach Bum Phillips. "I think he plays to his ability more than anyone else. To me, he's a winner from the bottom of his shoes right up to his helmet."

Staubach was the best runner, a master scrambler whose 2,264 yards (plus 20 touchdowns) still stands No. 8 on the team's all-time rushing list. Running had its consequences, though, as did a career total of 313 sacks, many caused by stubborn reluctance to dump a pass while he sought a big-play receiver downfield.

An accumulation of more than 20 concussions dating back to high school forced Staubach to retire at 37 after 11 NFL seasons. His major honors include four NFL passing titles, NFC Player of the Year (1971), five Pro Bowl nominations, MVP of Super Bowl VI and induction into the Pro Football Hall of Fame.

Unlike Meredith and Aikman, Staubach benefited from a ready-made roster. He first started in 1971 for a team that had lost Super Bowl V the previous year. Meredith experienced the pangs of a start-up franchise. The Cowboys of Aikman's 1989 rookie season, who went 1-15, weren't much better than expansion fodder.

Future Super Bowl victories aside, Aikman's finest hour lay in the rubble of '89 and coach Jimmy Johnson's dubious decision to start the raw kid without benefit of even modest support. The risk to young QBs who have no chance to succeed is permanent loss of confidence. Aikman went winless (0-11) before predictable injury put him out. But where others would buckle under the stigma of

a once pitiful 1-14 starting record, Aikman emerged
mentally tougher and more committed to win.

A ikman is the most precise of the quarterbacks. He fits with the quick-pass, micro-
second timing routes of his offense just as
Staubach meshed with the shotgun for-
mation the Cowboys dusted off in 1975. Meredith
ran the performance scale from spectacular to
erratic.

Aikman so far hasn't matched Staubach in pro-
ducing late rallies because it's not been necessary.
The Cowboys have emerged as a team that seldom
trails. They win from ahead instead of from behind and
have been less dependent upon comebacks inspired by
their quarterback.

However, Aikman stands above Staubach in terms of playoff success. His career 10-1 record and 104.3 rating in postseason is evidence that the bigger the game, the better he
plays. A career Super Bowl record 70 percent completion
percentage in three events confirms this view of Aikman.
Staubach by comparison finished 11-6 in playoffs (losing four
by a total of 12 points).

Another standard measuring rod is the ratio of touchdown passes to interceptions. The order for regular season
only: Staubach plus-44 in TDs to INTs, Meredith plus-24 and
Aikman plus-13 despite setting a club record in '95 by throwing 184 consecutive passes without a steal. Then again, Aikman wasn't needed to throw many scoring passes with Emmitt
Smith setting an all-time NFL mark of 25 rushing TDs.

Aikman would be an exceptionally accurate passer in any
era under any set of rules. The game he plays favors offense
and Aikman's skill thus is magnified. He holds the five top single-
season completion percentages in Cowboys history with a
high of 69.1 in 1993. At 29, his individual honors already
include five Pro Bowls, one All-Pro and the MVP Award
in Super Bowl XXVII.

With Aikman's career still a work in progress,
it's not easy to draw a definite conclusion. One
thing's for certain though: Of all the great
quarterbacks who have played in the NFL,
three proudly wore the blue and silver of
the Dallas Cowboys on their helmets. •

*Frank Luksa covered the Cow-*
*boys during each of the three*
*quarterbacks' eras and is*
*currently a sports columnist*
*for* The Dallas Morning News.

LAYNE MURDOCH

AIKMAN

By Roger Staubach (as told to Mickey Spagnola)

# a common pers

**By winning three Super Bowl championships, Troy Aikman has accumulated a massive following of admirers. Perhaps his biggest fan? None other than the Cowboys' Hall of Fame quarterback, Roger Staubach.**

at the beginning, it was the physical ability that I sensed. There was just something about him that said, hey, this guy is going to be a heckuva quarterback.

Part of what you see is how he throws the ball, but you don't get a chance to really see his character until he is thrown into the action.

That first year, the thing that I noticed, he really took a beating. But he never complained. He just got back up and did his job, and did it very well.

And the purity of how he threw the ball, with his strength and the velocity he threw it — and he does that with such great accuracy. There have been a lot of quarterbacks with very strong arms who really don't have his accuracy. Troy is amazingly accurate for the type of quarterback he is — a power thrower.

The big thing you saw happen for Troy to reach that championship level [is] the guy just wants to win; he works at it. He's not going to be satisfied with just one good season. He's going to give it the best he has every time he goes out and plays football.

And when you have that kind of talent, and the mental discipline to do that, well, few people have that. Michael Jordan's got it. The great ones have got it. The great ones like Troy who continue to say, 'Hey, I'm not going to sit here and rest on my laurels. I'm going to actually try and get better' is really tremendously important as far as mental discipline, and what that does is carry over to a team.

And Troy has that quiet leadership about him. I think he's a bit shy at times. I've gotten to know him, but he's honest. He's real.

Now when it comes to actually playing, my style was different than Troy's. I was a different type of player than Troy.

I ran more. I didn't have as good of a release as Troy. I had power behind the football, but Troy gets rid of it very fast.

But no matter the style, it really comes down to the ability to win and move the football on the field. Make the right decisions, and also be very, very competitive. As a quarterback, you've got to want to win with a passion and pay the price to do it. I think we have similar qualities there. And it's a honor for me to be compared to Troy. He's won three Super Bowls, and I did some good things, too.

Troy and I are similar in the passion to win, the competitiveness. And he is tough. He's as tough as any quarterback I've seen play. And I thought I was very tough — physically and mentally.

As far as style, we got it done differently. But as far as the competitiveness and being willing to pay the price to win — I'll tell you, there are a lot of guys out there who are not paying the price.

When I'm watching the Cowboys play, I just don't believe there's never a chance they're not going to score, as long as Troy Aikman is out there. That feeling is important, and I just don't think there is a better quarterback in the league than Aikman. As long as Dallas keeps Aikman healthy, they're going to be in every game they're playing.

I mean, I'm trying to be objective about it, but I just think this guy is that good. From the time he was a rookie, I just saw something special in him, and he has not disappointed me.

He has exceeded my expectations — and those were at a Hall of Fame level when I saw him. But he's just knocked the lights out. •

*Roger Staubach, who retired from the NFL in 1979, currently owns a real-estate firm in Dallas.*

*Mickey Spagnola is a freelance writer based in Dallas.*

pective

TROY AIKMAN

TROY AIKMAN

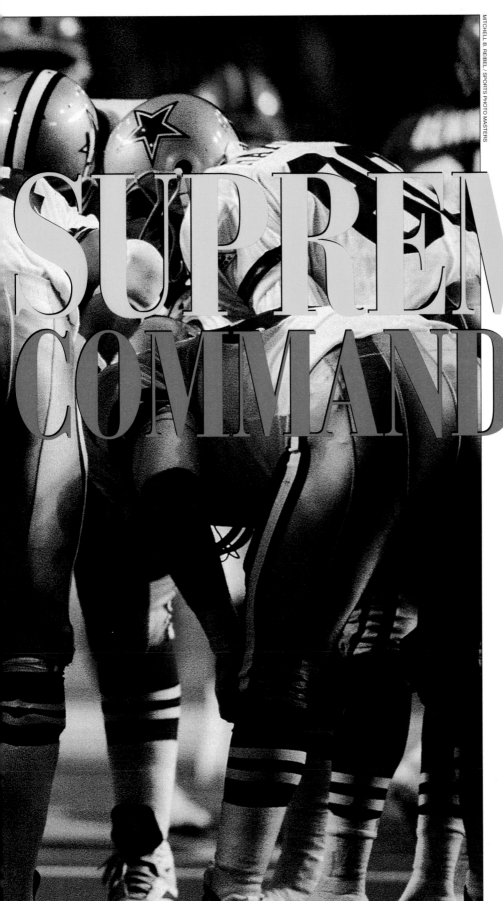

# SUPREME
# COMMANDER

By Mike Rabun

**Troy Aikman's
broad influence
as the leader
of the Dallas
Cowboys
extends
beyond the
typical protocol
of an NFL
quarterback**

In the few months following the 1992 NFL season, Troy Aikman was quite possibly the most sought-after athlete in the United States.

Not all that surprising, of course, since he recently had been anointed the Most Valuable Player of the Dallas Cowboys' first Super Bowl victory in 15 years.

Those with products to sell tapped on his door. Charitable organizations lined up with the hope of gaining an audience. And various media types also were desirous of having a word with the Cowboys' quarterback because he obviously was going to be the leading subject of many soon-to-be-released preseason publications.

It was during one of those visits with an inquiring scribe that Aikman discussed what he felt was a clear obligation.

"I recognize that I am going to have a lot of attention focused on me," Aikman admitted. "And I feel it is my responsibility to share it with my teammates.

"I get a lot of requests to speak and there is no way I can go to all of them. So if I can spread some of those things to other members of the team, I should certainly try to do it."

Seconds later, as if on cue, Cowboys guard Nate Newton strolled through the otherwise empty locker room, walked up to Aikman and thanked him for setting him up with a gig that probably had earned Newton some money.

This example illustrates that often vague but always vital quality known as "leadership."

Aikman is a leader, particularly when it comes to the Dallas Cowboys.

"A leader," explains Ernie Zampese, the Cowboys' offensive coordinator, "is a guy who can motivate other people to do the very best they can do, whether that is by example, or with words.

"You can look at somebody and just tell by the way he conducts himself and approaches the job and the work ethic he has. And Troy certainly has all of those qualities," Zampese says. "I think if you talk to anybody on this football team, it would be unanimous that if they looked upon one guy as the leader of the team, [Troy] is the one."

**Like all good leaders, Aikman stands tall in the heat of battle.**

Foremost, though, there must be a natural quality to what a leader does.

"It's all a matter of personality," continues Zampese, who's been coaching in the NFL since 1976. "Everybody does it their own way. And for a guy to be a true leader, he must be consistent. You

can't be changing how you do things."

In other words, somebody trying to be somebody he isn't doesn't have a chance.

"The guys would see through that in a second," Zampese claims. "You can't be a phony."

And how did these qualities take hold in Aikman? Well, it doesn't hurt that he consistently throws pinpoint-precise passes to his receivers year in and year out. Talent typically helps to define a leader.

But Aikman has developed more than talent. He has absorbed the lessons learned from a career spent in the harsh spotlight at the University of Oklahoma, UCLA and now with the Cowboys — perhaps the most followed athletic group in the history of the planet.

And the most important lesson is that to win in any

**Year after year, the Dallas Cowboys receive prodigious amounts of media attention — much of which is deftly handled by their star quarterback.**

team sport, personal concerns must be put aside. Aikman understands the team concept of football perhaps as well as anyone, and his actions have demonstrated that knowledge.

A couple of examples:

Early in the 1995 season, Cowboys owner Jerry Jones wanted to sign free agent Deion Sanders. To fit Sanders' prospective contract under the salary cap, Jones either had to cut a key player or alter the contract of a highly paid Cowboy.

Aikman stepped forward.

"If there was a guarantee that we would play in the Super Bowl if Deion Sanders played for the Cowboys, he could play here for my salary," Aikman said at the time. "I would play for free if we could have the third Super Bowl."

Aikman later suggested he might have been overstating the case by saying he would play for free. But those leadership qualities were paramount when Aikman, indeed, restructured his contract so that Sanders could become a member of the team.

Then, later in the season, when an assistant coach suggested to head coach Barry Switzer that he believed Aikman was singling out black teammates for criticism, and Aikman learned of the charge, the Cowboys quarterback saw to it that the matter did not

TOM DiPACE

spill into the public domain.

Leaders do not expose wounds by creating a stink in the media about something that can be dealt with internally.

During Super Bowl week, in fact, one of the more fascinating moments occurred when a reporter asked Aikman a question he felt was a bit too personal.

PETER READ MILLER

**Even during the off-season, Aikman leads by example, pushing himself with an intense conditioning regimen.**

"I'm not going to discuss that," Aikman said.

"Why not?" the questioner wanted to know.

"Just because you have a pad and pencil doesn't give you the right to know everything that goes on in our locker room," Aikman replied.

End of questioning.

Leaders know how to deal with such matters. And when the locker room intrigue Aikman had suppressed during the season came to light during Super Bowl week, his teammates stormed to his side as if they were rushing to the battlements.

Leaders also know how to adapt, which Aikman successfully has done.

In Dallas, Aikman has played for coaches who exhibit strikingly different working styles.

Aikman grew to like Jimmy Johnson's autocratic system. Early on, he recognized the benefits of Johnson's methods, which ultimately led the franchise

**Aikman supplies constant support and encouragement to his teammates, especially those directly responsible for keeping him injury-free.**

to two Super Bowl victories.

Accepting Switzer's laid-back approach was not easy for Aikman. But as he does with most situations, the unquestioned leader of the Cowboys thought it through, determined the best course of action and embarked upon it.

He did what was best for the team. And it might be

argued that because he did, the Cowboys eventually won their third Super Bowl title in four years and, in the process, earned Zampese the Super Bowl ring that had eluded him for so long.

Leaders, after all, also think about others. •

*Mike Rabun covers the Dallas Cowboys for United Press International.*

# rags

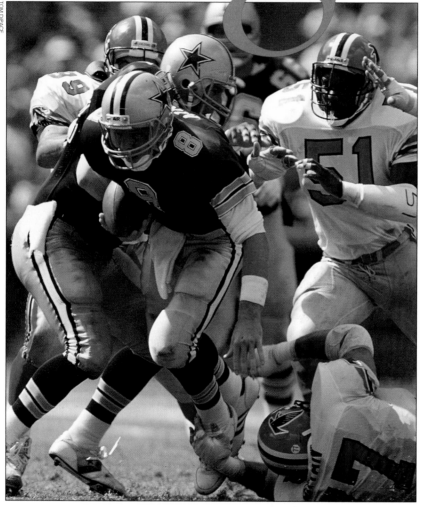

**After stumbling through a rocky start to his NFL career, Troy Aikman quickly elevated his game and reaped the rewards of a champion**

# to

By Denne Freeman

# Riches

Troy Aikman is a once-in-a-lifetime quarterback.

As an accomplished veteran, Aikman finds a way to win. He's a living training film with his model dropback and on-the-money throws. But the best thing about him is that he is a true competitor. Aikman will find a way to beat you even if it means he has to run, a sure ticket for defenders to inflict mayhem on his body.

If you wanted to nitpick, the worst you could say about him is that he doesn't grip the ball by the laces when he throws. For this reason, he sometimes has problems handling slick balls on cold, rainy days.

But rain or shine, Aikman is the kind of quarterback you want on your side in a Sunday war.

Life on the football field has not always been rosy for the seven-season veteran. Aikman was given every reason to fail because of his rocky starts in both college and professional football.

Aikman signed with Oklahoma because he thought coach Barry Switzer was switching to a passing offense. But after Troy broke his ankle during the early part of his sophomore season, Jamelle Holieway stepped in and quarterbacked the Sooners to a national championship with a wishbone offense.

Because Aikman wasn't a running quarterback, he didn't see himself in the Sooners' future. So with Switzer's blessing, Aikman transferred to UCLA, where his talents bubbled to the surface like an Oklahoma oil gusher.

By his senior season, Aikman was one of the most sought-after prizes of NFL scouts, who drooled at his size, smarts and throwing ability.

Dallas Cowboys coach Tom Landry, who had just suffered through a 3-13 season, said of Aikman, "I sure like the way he throws a football. This kid could be one of those franchise guys that turns around a program."

Landry never got to find out. New team owner Jerry Jones swept him out the door and brought in Jimmy Johnson, who drafted Aikman as the first overall pick in the '89 draft.

The first season under Johnson was quarterback hell for Aikman. The quarterback coach and offensive coordinator was Dave Shula, and he and Aikman never got on the same page.

The Cowboys offensive line was so porous that Aikman spent most of his time dodging defenders instead of looking downfield for his receivers.

In one game against the Cardinals, Aikman threw a touchdown pass and got knocked cold as he released the throw. He didn't get to see the play until weeks later in the films.

Aikman had difficulty reading the difference between zone and man defenses while on his back, and the Cowboys stumbled through a disappointing 1-15 season. Aikman, a rookie, was confused enough even when he had a chance to look a defense over. The second season was much the same.

Aikman continued to take a physical beating. Through his first two seasons as a pro, various injuries allowed

He's now accustomed to the trappings of Super Bowl glory, but the foundation of Troy's success was laid through years of dedication and hard work on the practice field with offensive coordinators Norv Turner and Ernie Zampese (right).

Aikman to take refuge on the sidelines for seven games. In the 25 games he did play in, he was sacked 58 times.

Then Norv Turner became the team's offensive coordinator.

Johnson took a recommendation from defensive coordinator Dave Wannstedt and hired Turner away from the Los Angeles Rams, where he was an assistant.

The union turned Aikman's career into one that someday will end in Canton, Ohio with his induction into the Professional Football Hall of Fame.

Turner introduced Aikman to the West Coast passing offense, a style that fits the quarterback's game perfectly. Turner shortened Aikman's drops and had him throwing timing passes. He boosted Aikman's confidence over the moon.

"The good thing when I arrived was Troy had played two years," Turner

*Aikman's poise in pressure-packed situations such as a Super Bowl is a stark contrast to the frequent befuddled and shell-shocked look of his early NFL years.*

says. "He had an understanding of how hard it was to play in the NFL. Troy also had Michael Irvin, tight end Jay Novacek, Emmitt Smith and a good upcoming group of offensive linemen.

They were talented but not successful.

"What Troy needed was someone to get everything working together," Turner continues. "Get them all going in the same direction. I brought in the system. They had been running a lot of routes with him holding ball. It was not conducive to good protection."

Turner went to work.

"I shortened the routes, cut down the steps on his drops, and based everything on quick timing. He was hit less and took fewer sacks. I mixed in an emphasis on the run game to utilize Emmitt's skills.

"Troy is suited for this kind of a game. It gave him something to hang

## Troy's Targets

The following is a breakdown of Troy Aikman's 119 career TD passes:
(98 regular season, 21 playoffs)

| | | | |
|---|---|---|---|
| 1989 | — 9 | 1992 | — 31 |
| 1990 | — 11 | 1993 | — 20 |
| 1991 | — 11 | 1994 | — 17 |
| | 1995 | — 20 | |

| | |
|---|---|
| Michael Irvin | 42 |
| Jay Novacek | 25 |
| Alvin Harper | 19 |
| Daryl Johnston | 10 |
| Emmitt Smith | 6 |
| Kelvin Martin | 5 |
| Kevin Williams | 3 |
| James Dixon | 2 |
| Steve Folsom | 1 |
| Bernard Ford | 1 |
| Dennis McKinnon | 1 |
| Tommy Agee | 1 |
| Derek Tennell | 1 |
| Alfredo Roberts | 1 |
| Scott Galbraith | 1 |
| Total | 119 |

his helmet on. Troy never lacked for confidence but this gave him something he really believed in. It gave him a jump start."

Turner says Aikman has improved even after he left Dallas following the '93 season.

"Troy is very intelligent," he says. "Very serious. Very studious. The last two years watching him on film I see him improving. He is doing little things like throwing the ball away [or] dumping the ball to Emmitt. He is a great decision maker."

Turner still laughs about the anti-Aikman faction that greeted him when he arrived in Dallas.

"A bunch of people asked me if I thought he could be a big-time quarterback," Turner says. "I told them 'You don't understand how good this guy is.'"

When Turner left to become the Redskins' head coach, Aikman was despondent.

"It was a special relationship between me and Norv Turner," Aikman says. "He taught me the finer points of the game. He turned me from a thrower into a passer. He was a great play caller. He always kept my confidence up. It hurt when he left."

But Aikman's luck continued. The Cowboys hired Ernie Zampese away from the Rams. Zampese taught Turner everything he knew. So, Zampese and Aikman were on the same page from the beginning.

"I hoped sometime in my career I would be fortunate enough to work with a quarterback like Troy Aikman," Zampese says. "What a dream to have a runner like Emmitt Smith, a receiver like Michael Irvin and a great quarterback like Troy."

Zampese, after 20 years in the business, earned his first Super Bowl ring when Dallas beat Pittsburgh in January. And Aikman took special pride

Aikman's ability to recognize different defensive sets and his quick thinking at the line of scrimmage have kept the Cowboys' offense one step ahead of its opponents.

in getting Zampese the piece of championship jewelery. "One of the biggest joys I got out of winning the Super Bowl was getting the ring for Ernie," Aikman says. "He had been in the business forever and never even gotten to the Super Bowl. That was special."

Through the tutoring of Turner and Zampese, Aikman has become one of

the most feared playoff quarterbacks in history. He has a 10-1 record as a starter in playoff games with the only loss coming at San Francisco in the NFC Championship Game two years ago.

He is the second highest rated passer in NFL postseason history. Aikman's rating of 104.3 is just behind that of the all-time leader, Green Bay's Bart Starr at 104.8.

"Troy Aikman has great technical form but he also is a strong competitor," Starr says. "This makes him very hard to beat."

Aikman is also the NFL's all-time leader in playoff completion average at 68.3 percent and yards per attempt at 8.65. He is 239 of 350 for 3,029 yards, 21 touchdowns and just nine interceptions.

Zampese: "I knew he was a great quarterback before I got here. To see him on the field at quarterback schools, I was so impressed at how quickly the ball came out. He threw it so straight all the time. His accuracy is unbelievable.

"He has size, intelligence and is very compact when he throws it," Zampese continues. "He competes and wants to win so badly. It just burns in

him. He's got everything. He's such a team guy and is really careful of what he does with the football so his team won't get beat by something dumb."

Zampese concludes: "I've never been around a guy like him. He's the best I've ever been around and I was around Dan Fouts, who made it to the Hall of Fame. He's the best quarterback in football today."

And for Zampese and Turner, Aikman just may have been that once-in-a-lifetime quarterback.    •

*Denne Freeman is the Texas sports editor for the Associated Press.*

## 1 Head

• Nov. 12, 1989 at Phoenix — On his first game back after missing five games with a broken finger (see below), Troy is knocked unconscious as he releases a 75-yard scoring strike to James Dixon. The touchdown puts Dallas up, 20-17, with 1:43 remaining in the game. Despite the severity of the hit, Troy misses no action.

• Jan. 24, 1994 vs. San Francisco — During the NFC Championship Game, Aikman suffers a concussion in the third quarter after driving Dallas to a 28-7 lead. He sits out the remainder of the game but returns in two weeks to lead the Cowboys to a Super Bowl victory.

• Oct. 23, 1994 at Phoenix — Cardinals linebacker Wilber Marshall violently blasts Aikman on the game's opening drive, giving Troy his second concussion in less than a year. Aikman stays in the game, however, and delivers a TD pass before leaving the game for good.

## 2 Shoulder

• Dec. 23, 1990 at Philadelphia — In the first quarter, Aikman separates his right shoulder after being knocked to the turf by an Eagles defender. Aikman undergoes surgery and misses the season finale at Atlanta.

## 3 Finger

• Oct. 1, 1989 vs. New York Giants — Aikman breaks his left index finger scrambling for a first down. After immediately leaving the game, Aikman does not step back out onto the field until six weeks later at Phoenix.

## 4 Hamstring

• Nov. 7, 1993 vs. New York Giants — A strained left hamstring interrupts one of the best statistical seasons of Aikman's career. Troy misses 2-1/2 games because of the injury.

# Wounded Warrior

**Troy Aikman's body has been dealt a substantial amount of punishment during his NFL career**

## 5 Right Knee

• Nov. 24, 1991 at Washington — Aikman sprains the lateral collateral ligament in his right knee during the third quarter. Aikman misses the final four games of the regular season and plays only sparingly in a backup role during a playoff loss at Detroit.

## 6 Left Knee

• Nov. 20, 1994 vs. Washington — Aikman sprains the medial collateral ligament in his left knee during the second quarter. Aikman spends the next two games on the sidelines before returning vs. Cleveland on Dec. 10.

• Nov. 12, 1995 vs. San Francisco — Aikman bangs his left knee hard onto the turf and severely bruises it as he is sacked by 49ers defensive tackle Dana Stubblefield during the first quarter. Although Aikman left the game and did not return, he returns to the starting lineup the following week at Oakland.

## 7 Calf Muscle

• Oct. 1, 1995 at Washington — After releasing a short pass on the Cowboys' opening drive, Aikman strains his left calf muscle and awkwardly falls to the ground without being touched. Aikman misses the remainder of the game but returns to throw for 316 yards one week later against Green Bay.

TROY AIKMAN

# bind
## the ties that

Through seven NFL seasons, Troy Aikman has worked with countless individuals, but just a select few have had an indelible impact on his career that he'll never forget. Aikman's relationships with them may be personal and friendly, or they could exist on a pure businesslike basis only. Whatever the style, Troy Aikman has teamed with the following five important individuals to bring out the best in the Dallas Cowboys and in himself.

## By Jean-Jacques Taylor

TROY AIKMAN

# troy and & emmitt smith

Troy Aikman was a good quarterback before running back Emmitt Smith arrived in Dallas.

Aikman's first two seasons may have indicated otherwise because he failed to win as a starter his rookie season and threw 38 interceptions his first two years as a pro. But make no mistake, Aikman was a good quarterback. Smith merely enabled Aikman to become a great quarterback.

"Michael Irvin used to sit on the bench and cry after games because he'd be so tired of losing," Pro Bowl guard Nate Newton remembers. "I told him that we had a good quarterback and a good receiver but we weren't going to do anything until we got a big-time running back."

Nate was right.

The Cowboys made one of the best moves in franchise history when they drafted Smith with the 17th pick of the 1990 draft. Emmitt gave Dallas a legitimate running attack and took pressure off Aikman.

Teams' ability to run the football often sparks NFL success. With eight defenders crowding the line of scrimmage and intent on stopping Smith, Aikman found it easier to hit receivers running free in the secondary.

Passing teams can win a lot of games, but fancy offenses such as the Run & Shoot haven't lead to many titles. For instance, Buffalo used its loosey-goosey K-Gun offense to make it to the Super Bowl four consecutive years. Each time, they returned to Western New York without the Lombardi Trophy.

Meanwhile, Dallas captured four consecutive NFC Championships and three Super Bowl titles in Smith's six seasons as a pro. It's no coincidence.

"Emmitt has meant a great deal," Aikman says. "Considering the pieces we had in place with Michael and then me, it's obvious we were missing a running game. That allowed us to put all of the pieces in place.

"Michael, Emmitt and I all rely on each other for our own individual success. This is not baseball, where you can put up some huge individual numbers and not have the team do well."

Smith won four NFL rushing titles in those first six seasons, setting an NFL record with 25 touchdowns in 1995. He's a cinch Hall of Famer whose skills could easily be taken for granted.

But Aikman doesn't take the running back's skills for granted at all.

The quarterback says Smith's running allows Dallas to control the ball and frequently score in the red zone.

"A lot of people talk about Emmitt not having breakaway speed, but he doesn't have to," Aikman says. "He's so powerful in his hips and thighs that he's hard to bring down. He keeps the defense honest. I never take him for granted because I know how difficult the game is."

# troy and &michael irvin

Despite their contrasting styles, Michael Irvin and Troy Aikman are the heart and soul of the Dallas Cowboys.

Irvin's charisma and zest qualify him as a leader. He goes by the moniker "The Playmaker" and drove a convertible Mercedes with those vanity tags during the '95 season. Aikman's known around the locker room as "The Godfather" because he's the symbolic head of the family.

Aikman drives a white blazer with tinted windows and prefers anonymity. He rarely makes mistakes, and his teammates respect his ability to play hurt and to perform at a high level when the pressure is most intense.

Aikman and Irvin get along so well partly because opposites attract. Plus, they've suffered together.

Irvin, drafted 10th overall in 1988, played on the 3-13 team his rookie season and on the 1-15 team of Aikman's rookie season. The struggles Aikman and Irvin faced during the early part of their careers gave the quarterback and receiver a true perspective of the level of competition in the NFL and the teamwork it would take to win. They promised each other things would be different — when they got some help.

Things are now different.

In the three seasons before Aikman, Irvin and Emmitt Smith became teammates, the Cowboys were 11-36, a .234 winning percentage. In their first three seasons together, they were 31-17 with a .646 winning percentage and two Super Bowl wins. In the next two seasons, Dallas went 28-9 with another Super Bowl triumph.

Of all the receivers Aikman has thrown to in his career, Irvin seems to be his favorite target. Aikman has connected with "The Playmaker" for 42 touchdown passes in their seven seasons together.

A strong work ethic also bonds the two. No one works harder than Irvin and Aikman. Some may work just as hard, but no one outworks them.

Irvin spends much of the off-season honing his skills and catching passes. Much of the time, Aikman is throwing them.

The sight's unusual. An All-Pro receiver running routes. An All-Pro quarterback throwing passes. Each practicing as though he's trying to make the team in training camp.

"I have a tremendous relationship with Michael," Aikman says "I admire what he has gone through and what he's come through to get to where he is, and I admire and respect his work ethic.

"I care deeply for Michael and what he means to this football team and what he means to me, and I let him know that as often as I can."

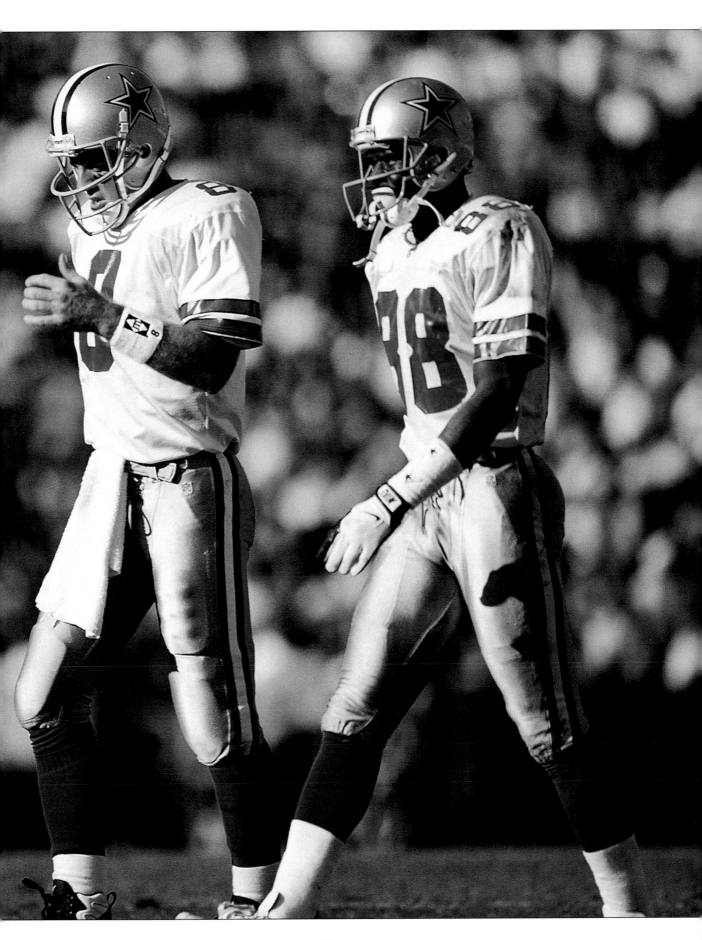

**TROY AIKMAN**

# troy and jerry jones

Jerry Jones and Troy Aikman have a relationship built on respect.

The owner respects the quarterback's ability to play hurt and excel in postseason play. The quarterback respects the owner's willingness to do whatever it takes to put the best team on the field.

"We have a very good relationship," Aikman says. "I don't have the win-at-all-costs mentality, and I don't know that Jerry does, but I've had a very positive, professional relationship since the day I signed here."

Teammates Emmitt Smith and Michael Irvin have a lot of pull within the organization, but no one has as much influence with Jones as Aikman does.

Becoming just the third quarterback in NFL history to win three or more Super Bowl championships has allowed him those privileges.

Aikman's eight-year, $50 million contract also gives him power. In this era of the salary cap and huge signing bonuses, players with long-term contracts such as Aikman's are valuable.

Their relationship has thrived through the years because Jones usually seeks Aikman's opinion before making a significant personnel move. And Aikman appreciates the gesture — even if situations don't always play out the way he would like them to.

Three years ago, Aikman volunteered to restructure his contract if it meant keeping guard Kevin Gogan. Jones declined and the Pro Bowler signed with the Raiders.

"There are times when Jerry has done things that I don't agree with, and that's certainly fine," Aikman says. "But we have a very open communication and my opinion is asked.

"When I have a concern, I express that to him. What I think or the way I think things should be done is not always the way it's done, but at least [my opinion's] heard."

But what Aikman says he appreciates most is Jones' willingness to provide him with the best teammates money can buy. The Cowboys had eight members of their offensive unit named to the Pro Bowl last season.

That kind of support, says Aikman, makes it easy to play.

"There are a lot of players out there, who don't play for owners that care about winning. All they care about is the bottom line," Aikman says. "Certainly, it's a big business and Jerry is as interested in the bottom line as anybody. But at the same time, he wants to win.

"As a quarterback, I don't think you can put a price on that because ultimately I'm going to be judged on winning and losing and not anything I do as an individual."

FOCUS ON SPORTS

TROY AIKMAN

# troy and jimmy johnson

Early in his career, Troy Aikman wondered if he would ever like Jimmy Johnson. He liked the coach's attitude and his intense desire to once again make the Cowboys a dominant team. But Aikman didn't like Johnson's attitude toward him.

After all, the Cowboys selected Aikman with the first pick overall in the 1989 draft. Then, they used a first-round pick to draft Steve Walsh in the supplemental draft.

Aikman resented the message issued by Johnson with the selection of Walsh. He had good reason. Walsh, also one of college football's top quarterbacks, played for Johnson at Miami. Aikman wondered if he would be able to compete on a level playing field.

Johnson did little to encourage the golden boy from UCLA in that first season. Aikman had little success as a rookie. But Walsh did, making the situation even more difficult.

However, Aikman apparently showed enough flashes to warrant a trade that sent Walsh to New Orleans early in the 1990 season.

"Jimmy and I struggled early," Aikman remembers. "I never questioned Jimmy's desire to win or how much it meant to him. I think he handled some things wrong. I felt like he could have been a little more up front about some things, but Jimmy has his reasons for the way he handled certain things. But at the time, I didn't think we could get along."

As the Cowboys became a team on the rise, Johnson began to see Aikman in a different light. He witnessed the emergence of a quiet leader.

After the Cowboys' first Super Bowl win, Johnson and Aikman decided to spend some time together. During casual conversations, they discovered they had quite a bit in common, especially their views on the committment to win championships.

Johnson, who loves tropical fish, even helped Aikman set up his own aquarium. Now, Johnson respects few players more than Aikman.

"Win or lose," said Johnson, prior to the Cowboys' 27-17 Super Bowl win over Pittsburgh, "I think Troy Aikman will go down as one of the great quarterbacks in NFL history."

The Super Bowl win secured Aikman's spot in history. And his relationship with Johnson is as good as it has ever been.

"Once he realized that I was as driven and dedicated to winning as he was, and it meant as much to me as it meant to him, then the relationship really flourished," Aikman says. "We have a tremendous relationship now, and I hated to see him leave. I enjoyed playing for him and I have a tremendous respect for his ability to coach football teams."

TROY AIKMAN

# troy and & barry switzer

Troy Aikman and Barry Switzer possess different styles and ideas in working with a football team.

Aikman likes order, intensity and a rigid-style of preparation. In essence, he prefers former coach Jimmy Johnson's approach to practice and games. Switzer is less rigid. Under his regime, players have more freedom and leeway.

Aikman, though, is quick to point out that more than one successful style exists. The Cowboys' 27-17 Super Bowl win over Pittsburgh provides evidence of that.

"I've said before that Barry and I have different approaches to the game," Aikman says. "That doesn't make one right or one wrong. They're just different."

But the two have a definite rift in their relationship. Aikman often suggests that the last couple of seasons haven't been as much fun as seasons earlier in his career. He declines, however, to specify why. As always, in Aikman's mind, the team remains more important than the individual.

During the Super Bowl, however, news of the Aikman-Switzer rift leaked to the public. For a three-week stretch during the season, Aikman and Switzer did not speak to each other.

Charges that Aikman criticized just black players sparked the conflict. New Oklahoma coach John Blake, who coached the Cowboys' defensive line the last three seasons, was accused of starting the rumors.

Blake pointed to specific incidents involving Aikman with receiver Kevin Williams and right tackle Erik Williams, both of whom are black.

Switzer apparently drew Aikman's ire by questioning him about the charges instead of defending him against the accusations. Without hesitation, the players rallied around their quarterback at the Super Bowl.

"There are eight black players on offense," said defensive end Charles Haley at the time. "So there's an 80 percent chance he's going to be mad at a black player."

Aikman gave Switzer the game ball after the Cowboys beat Green Bay to win the NFC Championship. It seemed to be a gesture of good will.

Although neither Aikman nor Switzer appear willing to compromise their styles, they've apparently accepted each other as winners and have learned to co-exist.

Winning — and winning often — has a tendency to bring out the best in all people, no matter their style.                                                    •

*Jean-Jacques Taylor covers the Cowboys for* The Dallas Morning News.

# Canvas Cowboy

In much the same way
Troy Aikman strives
for perfection on the
football field, inspired
artists employ their
brilliance in creating true
representations of Dallas'
lone star quarterback

Opie Otterstad

TROY AIKMAN

Dan Smith

Dan Palmer

# Douglas J. Meythaler

Amy Chenier

# child prodigy

Once known as "the new kid in town," Troy Aikman developed himself into an athletic star a small Oklahoma community won't soon forget

**By Jeff Sparks**

**a**s a 12-year-old boy, Troy Aikman weighed the advantages — and disadvantages — of two cities.

In Cerritos, Calif., he could ride his bike to the playground, meet friends, play ball and enjoy all of the advantages a suburb of 50,000 had to offer.

In Henryetta, Okla. — population 6,500 — he could . . . "slop hogs and haul hay!"

Troy's decision was an easy one. He, and his bike, would stay in California.

The problem was, it wasn't his decision to make. His father, Kenneth Aikman, had dreamed of owning a ranch. And now, the time seemed right for the move. Troy, his father, his mother, Charlyn, and his two sisters, Tammy and Terri, were off to Oklahoma.

A genuine smile accompanied Troy through each ritual of childhood, whether he was posing for a portrait . . .

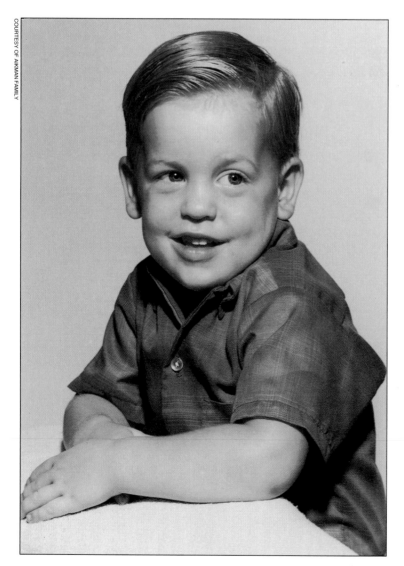

No more riding the bike to the playground for a pick-up game of basketball or to the baseball diamond for a sandlot game. His dreams of earning a baseball scholarship to the University of Southern California, and eventually, a spot in the major leagues — maybe even with the Dodgers — were ruined. His life now would revolve around feeding hogs and dodging twisters in tornado alley.

"I was 12 when my family moved here, and to be quite honest with you, I was not looking forward to it," Aikman recalls. "I grew up in a city where I could ride my bike to the gym and play basketball or to the schoolyard and play baseball like any other normal city kid.

"I'm not saying that's not normal in Henryetta, but we lived seven miles out of town on a dirt road with no close neighbors. It was a big shock to me. I couldn't understand why we moved."

The cows couldn't catch a fly ball if their hooves depended on it, and the hogs didn't make very good targets in the batter's box for working on a slider or a split-finger fastball.

That was it. Life was over.

"It was tough," Aikman says. "Even at that age I could see my athletic career falling apart."

Soon, however, things began to change.

"Once I got in school, I met some close friends, and after six months, I felt like I had lived here all my life," Aikman says. "I really came to appreciate the morals I learned in a small town on the differences between right and wrong. I lived in California longer than in Oklahoma, but I just identify much better with the people here."

Aikman excelled in all sports, and his dream of playing professional baseball nearly became a reality — straight out of high school.

Troy displayed a multifaceted game on the diamond. He hit above .600 his senior season and once struck out 13 consecutive batters against Seminole.

"Troy was a great team player," former Henryetta baseball coach Wiley Ryal says. "It was always the team first with him. He hit around .660 his senior year and it got to where nobody would pitch to him. There were a lot of scouts

looking at him, but Troy told me he wanted to play college football, so he was going to price himself out of the market in baseball. One scout told me that, too. He said they couldn't take a chance with that much money on a 17-year-old kid."

The New York Mets were set to select him straight out of high school in 1984. A scout even called the night before the draft to find out how much it would take to sign the rocket-armed pitcher/shortstop.

"Two hundred thousand," Aikman said.

To which the scout replied, "Good luck at Oklahoma," where Troy had signed a letter of intent to play football.

Five years later he would receive a $2.5 million signing bonus as the first player chosen in the 1989 NFL draft.

Oddly enough, his football career at Henryetta began not as a quarterback, but at fullback, in the eighth grade.

After a few weeks of taking a pounding up the middle, Troy decided football just wasn't his sport. He thought baseball would suit him better.

The future star of the Dallas Cowboys was set to give up the game that would make him one of the most recognizable and popular athletes in America.

Turns out, this wasn't his decision to make, either. His father wouldn't allow him to quit what he had started.

A year older and a year wiser, Troy let the coaching staff know the next season his true position was quarterback. Troy stepped into his new position as an immediate natural, leading his ninth-grade team to a 7-1 record with the only loss coming to Muskogee — a school much larger than Henryetta.

Aikman proved he had what it took to play quarterback that season and set a freshman record with a 94-yard bootleg pass during a come-from-behind win against Holdenville.

His size, however, meant he still would take a pounding on short yardage situations.

Troy was 6-1, 170, as a freshman and was flanked in the wing-T by running backs weighing from 110 to 129 pounds. On third or fourth and short, Aikman would shift back to the fullback position.

"I knew they couldn't stop him when we just needed a couple of yards," freshmen coach

**. . . or participating in Kindergarten graduation ceremonies.**

# henryetta hardship

Aikman's Game-by-Game High School Results:

**1981**
**Sophomore season (4-6)**
Henryetta 14, Checotah 6
Henryetta 25, Morris 15
Beggs 14, Henryetta 0
Catoosa 35, Henryetta 6
Seminole 27, Henryetta 13
McLoud 20, Henryetta 14
Bristow 35, Henryetta 18
Henryetta 20, Wewoka 0
Harrah 21, Henryetta 20
Henryetta 33, Tecumseh 18

**1982**
**Junior season (2-9)**
Okmulgee 27, Henryetta 20
Mannford 8, Henryetta 7
Morris 40, Henryetta 6
Beggs 27, Henryetta 6
Seminole 21, Henryetta 0

Okemah 35, Henryetta 21
Bristow 35, Henryetta 32
Hartshorne 28, Henryetta 21
Henryetta 43, Eufaula 36
Henryetta 16, Cheotah 0
**Playoffs**
Antlers 40, Henryetta 12

**1983**
**Senior season (6-4)**
Okmulgee 21, Henryetta 0
Henryetta 28, Mannford 27
Henryetta 21, Morris 14
Henryetta 34, Beggs 6
Henryetta 26, Seminole 21
Henryetta 33, Okemah 21
Bristow 43, Henryetta 13
Hartshorne 27, Henryetta 21
Eufaula 17, Henryetta 10
Henryetta 21, Checotah 10

Kent Lackey says about Aikman.

Troy also started at middle linebacker that year, where he proved he could be just as rough and tough without the football in his hands.

By his sophomore season, Troy had earned the respect of his coaches and was named the starting quarterback for the varsity team.

He led the Hens (who have since changed their mascot name to the Knights) to a 14-6 win over Checotah in the season-opener and then, to a 25-15 defeat of Okmulgee County rival Morris, the following week.

Finally, a team that had never won a playoff game in school history, was 2-0 and had title dreams riding on the shoulders of a rocket-armed 14-year-old.

# henryetta hero

Thirteen years removed from his hometown, Troy Aikman still dedicates his time and effort toward its well-being

Troy Aikman has gained fame and fortune as quarterback of the Dallas Cowboys. And the town of Henryetta, Okla., has benefited from his success.

Whether it's signing game jerseys for auctions, posters for charity or donating scholarships to high school students, Henryetta's favorite son has been there when needed — smiling and ready to lend a hand.

"Fortunately, with me being able to play for Dallas, I've been able to come back and try to put a little bit back in the community," Aikman says. "It's been very rewarding for me."

And for the community of 6,500 people.

"Troy is just a great individ-

ual," Henryetta High School football coach John Walker says. "He's all for Henryetta. Anything we need done, he has said he will help us do."

One of Aikman's biggest undertakings to help the school, and the community, was the construction of a 5,800 square-foot locker room/weightlifting facility at Henryetta's Cameron Stadium.

The entire community got behind the project. Troy donated the first $20,000 and Henryetta residents pulled together to raise the remaining funds. All the labor costs and much of the material were donated by local citizens and businessmen.

The project was completed in March 1993. An estimated crowd of 2,500 flocked into the high school football stadium for the dedication ceremony of the Aikman Fitness Center. Included in the crowd were Troy and then-Gov. David Walters, who proclaimed the day, March 6, 1993, "Troy Aikman Day" in Oklahoma.

"Henryetta is still a big part of me, and I try to help as much as I can," Aikman told the crowd. "I'm flattered that they named it after me and all that, but my contribution was no more significant than that of any other person who donated their time or money for the project. It really showed a lot about the community's pride to get behind it like they did and do something for the children."

*— Jeff Sparks*

But, like promising Henryetta teams before, this one also went bust. The Hens lost six of their next eight games to finish a disappointing 4-6.

The next season, Troy's team lost its first eight games before defeating Eufaula, 43-36, and Checotah, 16-0, in the final two games of the regular season. The back-to-back wins, however, qualified the Hens for the playoffs — a quirk that came with the new concept of four-team districts.

The new beginning didn't last long. Antlers drilled Henryetta, 40-12, in the first round of the playoffs.

As a senior, Aikman earned all-state honors while being courted to college by Barry Switzer at the University of Oklahoma and by Jimmy Johnson at Oklahoma State University.

Aikman's abilities were obvious. He could throw the ball a country mile and was also an effective scrambler.

Henryetta finished 6-4 his senior season and just missed the playoffs (the Oklahoma Secondary Schools Activities Association scrapped the four-team districts and went back to eight-team districts that season).

Through his three-season high school career, Aikman accumulated more than 3,200 yards and 30 touchdowns passing and more than 1,500 yards and 15 touchdowns rushing.

Despite the success, Aikman kept a low-key approach.

"In high school, he was a really quiet kid," Aikman's football coach Billy Ray Holt says. "Certainly so when he was starting as a sophomore and there were a lot of seniors.

"He was not really an outgoing leader, he just did it by showing how it was done. He wasn't real vocal about it."

Although his high school record was less than impressive, The Henryetta Hummer would have the last laugh — three Super Bowl titles and counting with the Dallas Cowboys.

Former Henryetta High School principal Danne Spurlock may have summed up Aikman's transition from the farm in Henryetta to his current high-profile status the best:

"Troy was always just a good ol' country boy. Now he's a rich one."  •

*Jeff Sparks is the sports editor at the* Henryetta Daily Free-Lance.

Just like the high school football jersey he would later wear, Troy proudly displayed the No. 10 as he rode his bicycle throughout Henryetta. Now it's the town that proudly recognizes its favorite son.

By Thomas Bonk

# big
# man
# on campus

Putting a rocky start to his college football career behind him, Troy Aikman
transferred to UCLA and immediately
started 'Bruin' up success

about the only thing they knew about Troy Aikman when he arrived on the campus of UCLA at Westwood is that the quarterback liked chewing tobacco and didn't like running the wishbone offense.

Actually, UCLA football coach Terry Donahue didn't care if Aikman dipped dandelions or chewed asphalt.

Donahue just needed one look at the kid who wanted to transfer from Oklahoma, and he knew something special had just dropped in his lap.

But that's getting ahead of the story. The tale of how Aikman wound up wearing UCLA powder blue and gold

**Aikman struggled in the pressure-filled atmosphere at Oklahoma.**

**He knew little of Troy Aikman before the quarterback transferred from Oklahoma, but UCLA coach Terry Donahue's good fortune became apparent immediately.**

began with a phone call.

"I'm sitting in my office and the secretary says Barry Switzer is on the phone," says Donahue, now the top college football commentator for CBS television.

"He said, 'Hey, I want to run something by you. We got a great one here.' Well, I hadn't heard of Troy before. Switzer just said he needed to transfer. The guy is a great player and he'd had enough of them to know one.

"And so Troy came here to UCLA," Donahue continues. "And the first time I saw him throw, I knew he had a great arm and that we had

a great player."

The rest is part of UCLA history, one with more than its share of riches in the quarterback department — Bob Waterfield, Billy Kilmer, Gary Beban, Mark Harmon, Tom Ramsey, Rick Neuheisel and Steve Bono.

After red shirting his

first season because of transfer eligibility rules, Aikman led the Bruins to back-to-back 10-2 records and consecutive bowl victories in 1987 and 1988.

As a junior, Aikman completed 178 of 273 passes and threw for 2,527 yards and 17 touchdowns. He also quarterbacked UCLA to a 20-17 victory over Florida in the Aloha Bowl, completing 19 of 30 passes for 173 yards in the defensive struggle.

Fully comfortable with the system, Aikman truly asserted himself during his senior season.

Aikman completed 228 of 354 passes for school-record totals of 2,771 yards and 24 touchdowns. This time, UCLA drew an invitation to the Cotton Bowl, where the Bruins held Arkansas to just 42 net yards and won, 17-3. Aikman was named the game's MVP after completing 19 of 27 passes

RICHARD MACKSON / SPORTS ILLUSTRATED

JERRY LODRIGUSS / SPORTS ILLUSTRATED

# cotton crop

After monitoring his development and growth, the hometown Dallas Cowboys harvested UCLA quarterback Troy Aikman shortly after his MVP-winning performance in the Cotton Bowl

i t was quite a familiar scene.

Dallas Cowboys coach Tom Landry and Cowboys personnel director Gil Brandt were standing on the sidelines of Texas Stadium just after Christmas of 1988. The scene had been repeated thousands of times. But there was something unusual about this occasion.

There was no NFL game in progress, nor were the Cowboys practicing. The UCLA Bruins were working out, preparing for their Cotton Bowl matchup with the Arkansas Razorbacks.

So why were Landry and Brandt present?

They were there for one reason — to scout UCLA senior quarterback Troy Aikman. The Cowboys, by virtue of their 3-13 record in 1988, had the No.1 pick in the upcoming NFL draft and were prepared to make Aikman their man. They told Aikman so.

"It was very understood that Troy was going to be the first pick of the Cowboys," says former UCLA coach Terry Donahue.

Although Landry was replaced by Jimmy Johnson before Aikman became a Cowboy, all parties knew that Aikman would soon be wearing the Cowboys' lone star.

"It made so much sense," Donahue says. "The Cowboys were in desperate need of a quarterback, he was an Oklahoma boy and he had a lot of country-Texas style in him.

"I'll tell you, our practices became an event."

Despite the overwhelming pressure to perform well for the Dallas football fans, Aikman came up big in the Bruins' 17-3 win over the Southwest Conference champs. In throwing for 172 yards on 19-of-27 passing, Aikman earned the game's MVP Award and reassured the hometown Cowboy fans that he would be a viable No. 1 pick.

Aikman wound up signing a six-year, $11.2 million contract. The sum was the most ever spent on an NFL rookie.

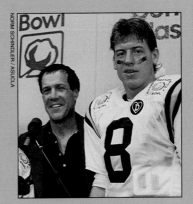

It was money well-spent. "He's been a fantastic pick," Donahue says. "He's taken two different types of Cowboys teams to three Super Bowls."

And no doubt, if the Cowboys had to do it all over again, they would not change a thing.
— *Thomas Bonk*

**Donahue and Aikman capped their three-year relationship with a win in the '89 Cotton Bowl.**

---

for 172 yards and one touchdown.

Aikman accepted national recognition as a consensus All-American, who also was honored with the Davey O'Brien Award — annually presented to the nation's top quarterback.

Personal success aside, winning has always been the top priority for Aikman.

Throughout Aikman's two seasons as the Bruins' quarterback, UCLA was regarded as a powerhouse not only in the Pac-10 Conference, but nationwide as well. Sans a three-week period early in Aikman's junior season, UCLA maintained a constant top-10 rating in the national polls, winning 20 of 24 games. The Bruins' No. 1

rating for two weeks during the '88 season was Donahue's first and only as UCLA's coach and the school's first since 1967.

It was a great success story for both Aikman and UCLA, and one which Donahue remembers fondly.

"If it hadn't been for Barry Switzer and the phone call he made, we never

would have got him," Donahue says.

Aikman was born in West Covina, Calif., but he grew up in Henryetta, Okla., which is much further from Los Angeles than a punt, pass and kick. Being recruited by Oklahoma was a childhood dream for Aikman, just as it is for each football-loving kid in the state, where the school's fight song "Boomer Sooner" is a lullaby.

Aikman spent two years with the Sooners, but didn't play much as a freshman because Danny Bradley was the star quarterback. And Aikman played in just three games in 1985 because of a broken ankle.

His statistics at Oklahoma are very un-Aikman-like, not at all similar to his success as a schoolboy at Henryetta. There, he threw

**Though best known in college for his passing, Aikman also proved himself nimble afoot.**

for 3,208 yards and 30 touchdowns and ran for 1,568 yards and 15 touchdowns through his three-season varsity career.

Aikman started off at OU as a fourth-string quarterback and probably was on track to be red shirted when he moved up in a hurry.

Before the Kansas game, Bradley got hurt and his backup was declared academically ineligible. Aikman won the starting job by outperforming the No. 3 quarterback in practice.

Aikman started, but had three passes intercepted and Kansas won, 28-11.

"I didn't want to come out of the dorm after that game," Aikman recalls.

As the team's sophomore starter, Aikman completed 27 of 47 passes for 442 yards and one touchdown before breaking his ankle in Week 4 against the Miami Hurricanes.

With Aikman on the shelf, the Sooners converted to a wishbone offense to accommodate freshman quarterback Jamelle Holieway, the new starter. Holieway capitalized on his opportunity by leading the Sooners to a national championship. At that point, Aikman real-

ized he needed a clean start with another school.

"At Oklahoma, you worry about what the media and the fans think about you all the time," Aikman says. "There's just so much emphasis on football back there. If you have a bad game it's like you're not a good person."

Donahue says Aikman also considered transferring to Arizona State and Miami. Aikman gave Miami special consideration because Hurricanes coach Jimmy Johnson was at Oklahoma State when he recruited Aikman out of high school.

**Troy Aikman seized his opportunity to shine in front of Dallas fans with an MVP performance in the '89 Cotton Bowl.**

But the deciding factor with Aikman may have been UCLA's pro-style offense, which involved passing the football more than running it.

Rick Neuheisel was a graduate assistant on Donahue's staff the season Aikman had to redshirt. The big blond kid became the pet project of Neuheisel, now the acclaimed young head coach at Colorado.

Aikman was a willing student and a quick study. Neuheisel versed him in the UCLA offense, and drilled him on his footwork with the play-action and the drop-back pass.

Donahue was very impressed with Aikman's progress.

"Troy was the only guy we've ever had who would hit 20 out of 20 passes in a skeleton drill," Donahue says. "Maybe people don't know how great that is, but some guys couldn't complete 20 passes throwing against just air.

"The ball was just so much on target. The receivers didn't so much as catch it as they did get hit by it."

In his first few months as a transfer, Aikman spent most of the time just getting used to his new surroundings.

"I got to know the guys who weren't on the traveling squad," Aikman says. "We'd do something on the weekends to occupy our time — pickup basketball, golf. They were lazy weekends. I'd always rather do something."

Donahue coached at UCLA for 20 years. He had seen a lot of great players come and go, but he never had seen anyone that quite matched up to Aikman. In Donahue's opinion, there was only one blemish on Aikman's stay at UCLA.

"It's just that Troy never beat USC," he says. "That sticks in his craw."

Donahue also says that as good as Aikman was, he wasn't a finished product when he left Westwood.

"When we had him at UCLA, he was in the developmental stage," Donahue recalls. "He was just learning. But look at the highlights of Troy's career — 20 victories, two years, two bowl games, No. 1 ranking for a while.

"But there's more to him. Troy is one of the most reachable superstars I've ever been around. He was nice to everybody. He was quiet, but forceful — an excellent leader.

"A lot of transfers, a lot of so-called superstars have a big wind behind them," Donahue continues. "Troy led by his talent. It thrust him into a superstar position. He let his talent speak for itself."

At UCLA, they will speak words of praise for Troy Aikman for a very long time. •

*Thomas Bonk is a sportswriter for the* Los Angeles Times.

Troy Aikman's
resounding success
on the football field
has translated into
numerous opportunities
on Madison Avenue

**W**alk up to a Coke machine, and there's Troy Aikman poised to throw a pass.

Drive down the highway, and there's Troy Aikman on a billboard, telling you to "Get Real" on behalf of Logo Athletic.

Walk through the health-food store, and there's Troy Aikman on the MET-Rx promotional display.

Turn on the TV set, and there's Troy Aikman promoting Chief Auto Parts.

And if you just happen to be in Dallas/Fort Worth Metroplex, turn on

That's what happens when you play for the Dallas Cowboys and combine success with this 'All-American-boy' image Aikman has managed to preserve since leaving his schoolboy days in Henryetta, Okla.

Not only has Aikman led the Cowboys to an unprecedented three Super Bowl titles in four seasons, but his persona as a laid-back and honest sports hero has rocketed his appeal across the board.

Troy sells — from the sports-

# COMMERCIAL

# SUC

By Mickey Spagnola

the radio and Troy Aikman will describe this weekend's special at The Troy Aikman Auto Mall.

The Dallas Cowboys Pro Bowl quarterback is turning up everywhere these days. After just seven seasons in the NFL, Aikman has become a national marketing giant.

"He is at the elite level," says Steve Schreyer, Aikman's new marketing agent. "He is one of the two or three most marketable football players."

minded audience to the health conscious, from the Madison Avenue board rooms to monkey-wrench guys working on their own cars.

Simply put, Troy Aikman's appeal is universal. Many of the products Aikman represents may not have much to do with football, but they are products (and companies) that he believes in and feels comfortable with.

"I'm pretty selective," Troy says about choosing a company to represent.

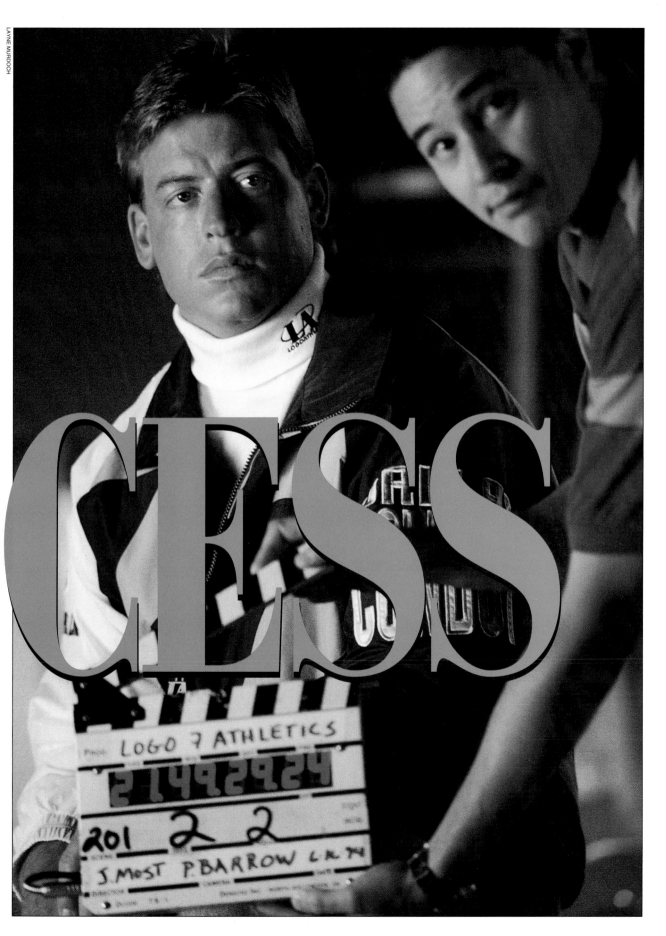

**LOGO 7 ATHLETICS**

2-444924

201  2  2

S.MOST  P.BARROW  CA 74

"I only do deals with people I feel good about. You can go out — if you're interested in it — and work pretty hard all off-season doing a lot of different deals, small deals and make a lot of money.

"But I really enjoy my time off. The money is not what drives me. So what I do is pick three, four, five major deals, and just focus my energies on those and do the commitment I have for them and

leave the rest alone for the most part.

"And then I try to have good relationships with those companies I do the endorsements for," Aikman continues. "For me, it goes beyond, 'Here is what we want to pay you and here is what we want you to do.' I want to have a relationship with these people."

So Troy not only knows the president of Logo Athletic, he considers him one of his good friends. He knows the people at Coca-Cola and Nike.

And because he does not believe in overkill, Aikman says he turns down about 90 percent of the offers he's given.

For Aikman, who's at the height of his national appeal and popularity, developing into a marketing mogul hasn't become a priority. That's why his endorsement list is, well, rather modest.

Among the companies he regularly represents are Logo Athletic, Coca-Cola, Nike, Chief Auto Parts, Score Board, MET-Rx, Acme Brick, Williams Entertainment and, of course, The Troy Aikman Auto Mall, his Fort Worth car dealership. For MET-Rx, Aikman is the nutrition drink-mix company's main spokesperson. And for Nike, as Schreyer puts it, "Troy is probably their top paid football player if you don't count Deion [Sanders]."

Needless to say, companies turn to Aikman for some immediate R&R —

**It's different from the pressure he faces on the football field, but Troy Aikman handles commercial studio shoots with similar poise.**

Recognition and Response. Companies want to identify with Aikman's appealing looks, as well as his leadership qualities and his toughness.

"Some like the rebel image," Schreyer says. "If so, that's not going to be Troy."

Some might like their main spokesperson to be available year-round, to continue putting time in on commercials or photo shoots. Well, then that's not going to be Troy, either. And even though "guys like Troy can make as much off the field as he does on," Schreyer says, you guessed it — that's not Troy, either.

When Aikman's popularity really started to kick in nationally following his MVP performance in Super Bowl XXVII, he wasn't very interested in spending his valuable off-season time doing what it takes to endorse a product.

"I used to not like doing [commercials]," Aikman admits. "I hated doing it. I hated the photo shoots. I hated doing the commercials. I just didn't enjoy that. I think that the reason was my level of expectations wasn't realistic. I thought you could go in, and do a commercial in an hour."

Aikman, a firm believer in regimen and punctuality, quickly discovered that was not the case in show business.

"But over the years, having done a lot of them, now I go in with the frame of mind saying, 'Hey this is going to take eight hours,' or however long you're going to be there," Aikman says. "So now, just over the last year, I've begun to enjoy that process more."

Unlike many athletes, Aikman understands the reasons behind his popularity and why he's held in such high regard by national corporations. He must maintain his status as one of the top quarterbacks in the league, and Dallas must remain a successful team. If the Cowboys stumble to mediocrity or

**Shortly after the Cowboys' Super Bowl XXX victory, Aikman made a guest appearance on *The Tonight Show* with Jay Leno and opened a Chevrolet dealership in Fort Worth, Texas.**

if his performance drops off, then so will the endorsements.

"The important thing to realize, and I think a lot of players fail to realize this, is no one wants me to endorse a product for them just because they think I'm a nice guy, if they think that at all," Aikman says. "Any activities or involvements you might have in the off-season that help you earn extra money, they are all dependent on how we do as a football team. And I've never lost sight of that.

"So I don't ever get to the point where I'm doing things that take away from my preparations to get myself ready to play or to get myself prepared for a season. Because once we're not doing well on the football field, all that will stop, believe me.

"And some players who enjoy success on the field, then think that trans-

lates into endorsements off the field and they lose sight of why those endorsements came," Aikman continues. "And [when] all this other off-the-field activity starts to take away from their preparations, they slowly but surely aren't the player they once were."

Confusing image with reality is a problem that may hit some players but will never blindside Aikman. •

*Mickey Spagnola is a freelance writer based in Dallas.*

# A
# Special
# Calling

By Jean-Jacques Taylor

Each and every Sunday, Troy Aikman helps his teammates win football games. But the best help that the Cowboys' quarterback typically delivers is to needy children and charities nationwide.

Countless stories exist about Troy Aikman's prowess on the football field.

Fans tend to expect no less from the starting quarterback of the Dallas Cowboys, who have won an unprecedented three Super Bowl championships in the last four seasons.

But it seems as though there are just as many stories about Aikman's prowess when it comes to charity work.

But Aikman doesn't just donate money, he takes a personal interest in the projects he supports.

"I do it primarily because I have the ability to do it," he says. "As far as my own foundation, I try to raise money for some disadvantaged kids. I get kind of embarrassed by some of the attention by the charity work that I do because there are far more players in the NFL that do benefits and help raise money than don't. I'm not any different than a lot of other players."

Knowing there would be a lot of demands for his work with charities, Aikman and his agent, Lee Steinberg, created The Troy Aikman Foundation in 1992.

"It seemed like it would make more sense to have my own foundation so I could direct my energies toward the things I wanted to do," Aikman says. "There are a lot of people who fall through the cracks and aren't able to get any help. We wanted to help them, that's why we chose

Helping kids. . .one dream at a time.

THE
Troy Aikman
FOUNDATION

the motto, 'One dream at a time.'"

Aikman takes pride in the projects and organizations he supports. He attends functions whenever possible and often donates something more valuable than money — time.

"I'm really not interested in the publicity of doing something for the attention. I'm interested in the results," he says. "If I'm supporting something, then I'm supporting it. I don't just want to cut a check. I like to get involved."

One of Aikman's biggest projects is with Children's Medical Center in Dallas. Aikman, who has a special affinity for children, has been involved with the hospital for several years.

Aikman has donated about $250,000 toward the construction of a playroom called Aikman's End Zone. The playroom will provide a place for hospitalized children to play and have fun. Through computer technology, the children also will have the opportunity to interact with other kids around the country who have similar illnesses.

"This will be very good for children who are here for a long period of time," says George Farr, CEO of Children's Medical Center. "For a child, two days can seem like forever,

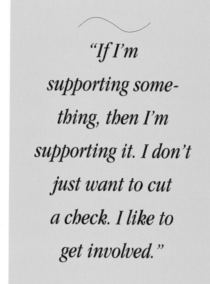

*"If I'm supporting something, then I'm supporting it. I don't just want to cut a check. I like to get involved."*

Troy Aikman

and we have some kids who are here for as long as 30 days. Even though a lot of good things happen during their stay, we want to do every little bit we can to make the life of a child a little better."

Which is exactly why Aikman thinks Aikman's End Zone will be such a hit.

"While the kids are in the hospital, they can go in the playrooms and they can have fun and forget their own problems," Aikman says. "I'm pretty fired up about it because you can go in there and see the impact being made."

Because the rooms would be easy to duplicate, Aikman would like to see similar rooms constructed in hospitals in the other 29 NFL cities. In San Francisco, for instance, one could be called Young's End Zone or Rice's End Zone. In Miami, it could be Marino's End Zone.

The name isn't important, Troy says. The help it provides is.

"So many times we go out and do charity work and you know you're raising money for something and you know it's a good cause," Aikman explains, "but you don't walk away with a real sense of satisfaction. With something like this, those who donate money can physically see where the money is going and how it's helping."

Not only will children be able to interact with other children around the country, but at times they'll have the opportunity to visit with Troy himself. With assistance from Steven Spielberg's Starbright Foundation, computer and video equipment is being installed in Aikman's home, which will allow him to talk on-line with kids from across the country. The project also involves some virtual-reality components, says Aikman, which should

**Troy may not be able to provide a doctor's care for children, but he is capable of brightening their day and making them feel like the star.**

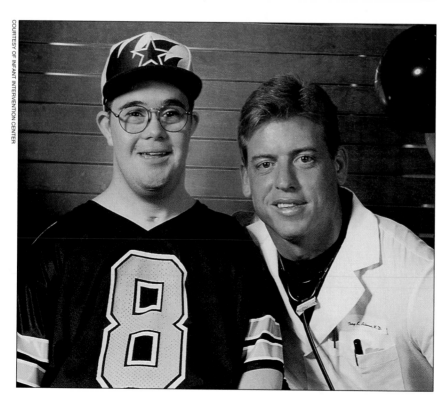

really give the children quite a charge.

"I really think it will be a neat deal because it will be set up so that when I have some free time, I can get on-line and communicate with these kids who are sick or in hospitals and just chat with them," Aikman says.

Aikman is merely continuing the legacy former Cowboys quarterback Roger Staubach started in the '70s and carried forth throughout his playing career.

"As good a football player as he is, Troy is even a better person," Farr says. "It's just that being a football player gives him an opportunity to teach people some things about life.

"Some athletes don't want to be role models, but in a lot of cases a person like Troy can teach kids a lot more than other people because he can get their attention."

Aikman, who has several nieces and nephews, enjoys

*"The first thing Troy said was that she had beautiful eyes. He didn't even notice her braces. That's when I knew he was a rare individual, and in my eyes he became Saint Troy."*

Phala Finley, executive director of the
Infant Intervention Center of Irving

Troy and many of his Dallas Cowboys team-mates provided support and encouragement to Gov. Frank Keating and the people of Oklahoma following the tragic Oklahoma City bombing in April 1995.

doing special things for kids. Children, he says, are just looking for a friend.

Perhaps that explains why Aikman went out of his way to impact one little girl's life. A life that was brightened by Troy's extra effort.

The girl, a patient at Children's Medical Center, didn't know Aikman and a few of his teammates were scheduled to visit the hospital one day. She did, however, tell some members of the hospital staff that, "If I could see Troy Aikman, I'd feel a whole lot better."

When the players arrived at the hospital, some members

of the staff took Aikman to see the little girl. But she had gone to get her eyes examined in another part of the hospital. Not wanting her to miss out on the fun, Aikman ventured out to find her.

"When she saw him, he was startled because she was so surprised to see him," Farr says. "The little girl, who was in a wheelchair, looked at Troy and said, 'I love you.'

"It just shows you the impact that people like Aikman can have on lives. It was a neat experience that that little girl will never forget."

**Aikman says that his charitable activities are as rewarding for him as they are for the children involved.**

> *"The little girl, who was in a wheelchair, looked at Troy and said, 'I love you.' It was a neat experience that that little girl will never forget."*
>
> George Farr, CEO of Children's Medical Center

Phala Finley, executive director of the Infant Intervention Center of Irving (Texas), has known Aikman since his rookie season. She recalls a similar experience with Aikman three years ago.

"We were talking and a little girl wearing leg braces walked in," says Finley. "The first thing Troy said was that she had beautiful eyes. He didn't even notice her braces. That's when I knew he was a rare individual, and in my eyes he became Saint Troy."

Aikman's charity assistance has not been limited to just children. Shortly after the Oklahoma City bombing in April 1995, Aikman and many of his Dallas Cowboys teammates provided on-the-scene support to the people

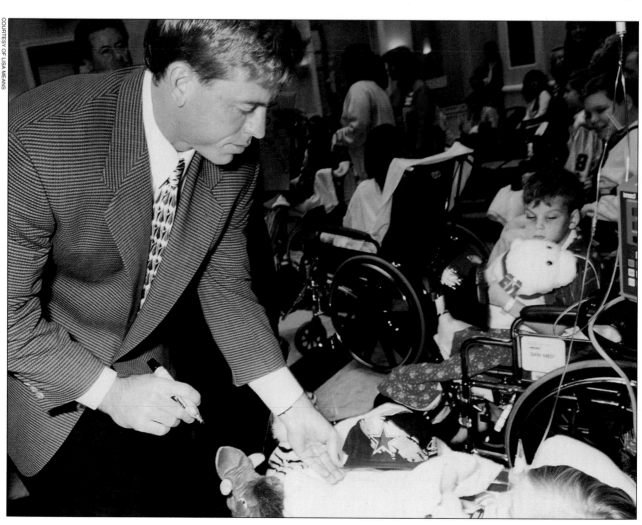

COURTESY OF LISA MEANS

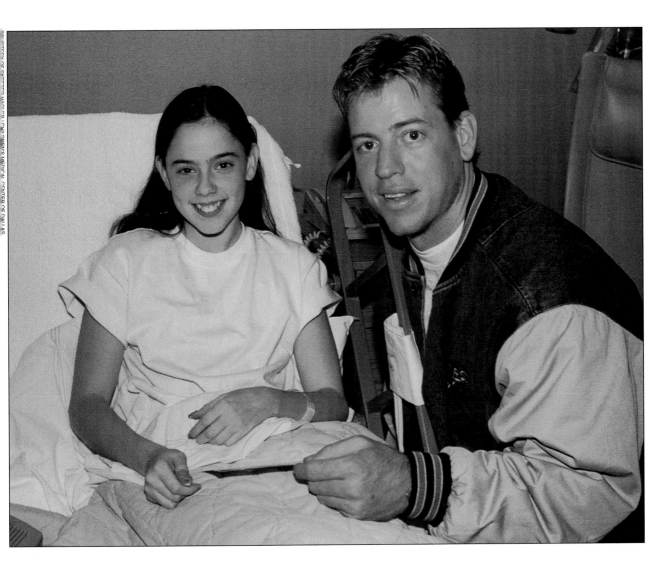

who were directly affected by the tragedy.

Through his foundation, Aikman also donated $10,000 to the bombing relief fund and became the honorary co-chairman for "Hitting For The Heartland," a fund-raising celebrity softball game played in Oklahoma City.

Aikman's efforts beyond the normal call of duty don't surprise Tom Whiteknight, Aikman's teammate and roommate at UCLA and one of his closest friends. Aikman, Whiteknight says, always has been cognizant of how he can help others.

"He has always taken the extra time to sign an autograph or help someone out," he says. "He's always very quiet about the things that he does because he doesn't want people to know that he's doing them."

> "He has always taken the extra time to sign an autograph or help someone out"
>
> Tom Whitknight,
> Aikman's friend

**Troy's ability to lift a patient's spirits is a special gift, indeed.**

Troy's mother, Charlyn, who helps run The Troy Aikman Foundation, says her son always tries to take that approach with his off-the-field endeavors.

"He's like that in every area of his life," she says. "He would love to play football, go home and have no one know who he is. He's just a real private person by nature."

As private as he may be, Aikman still is willing lend a hand and be a generous hero to those who need his help the most.          •

*Jean-Jacques Taylor covers the Cowboys for* The Dallas Morning News.

TROY AIKMAN

STAR LIGHT...

# STAR BRIGHT

From any angle, Troy is a superstar on and off the field. Our special photo essay puts on an all-out blitz to reveal the man behind the facemask.

TROY AIKMAN

# KID'S STUFF

Growing up, Troy performed all the simple rituals of childhood — a pony ride, the first day of school (with sisters Tammy and Terri), portrait sittings and Little League baseball.

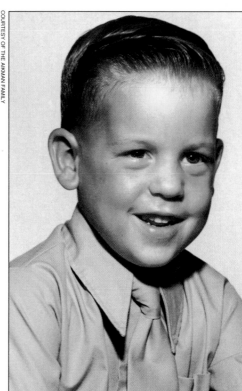

**TROY AIKMAN**

# AT HOME ON THE RANGE

Watch out, Redskins! This true-to-life Cowboy fits the image well, whether he's donning his blue & silver uniform or the real cowboy attire.

PETER READ MILLER

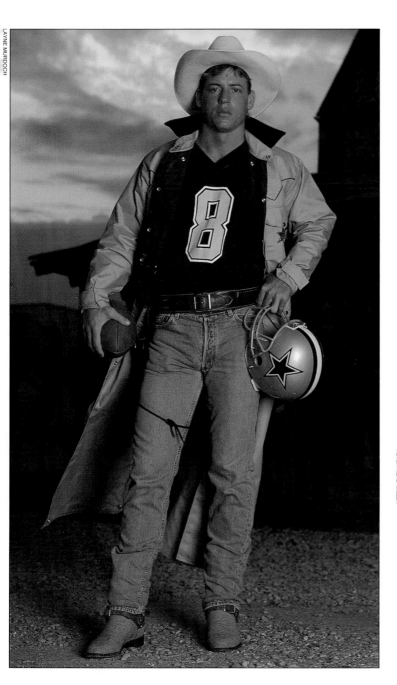

**TROY AIKMAN**

# STAR OF THE SHOW

There's no bigger stage than the Super Bowl. And no one recently has played the lead role better than Aikman, who has led Dallas to three Super Bowl triumphs in the last four seasons.

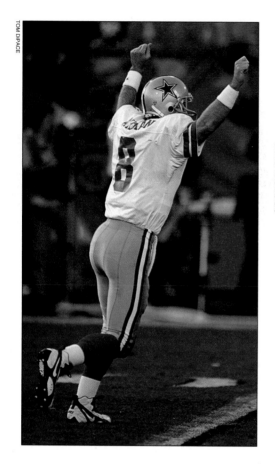

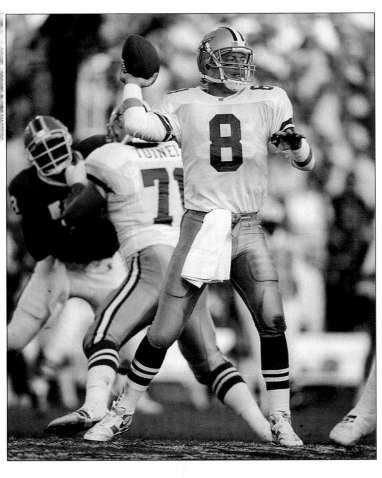

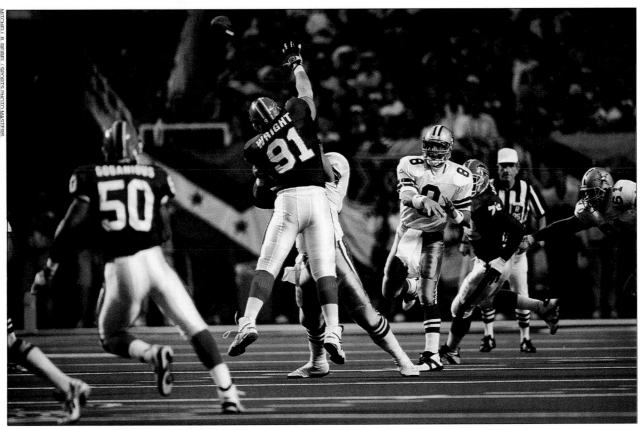

TROY AIKMAN

# HERO

By David Barron
Photography by
Gail Docekal

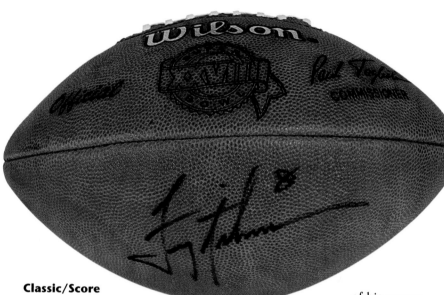

**Classic/Score Board recognized Aikman's value even before he won a Super Bowl, signing him to an exclusive autographed memorabilia contract in 1993.**

phone card at $1,800, a 1995 Pacific Gridiron Gold at $600, some of the recent Playoff and Collector's Edge Excalibur chase cards and several of the old Action Packed 24K cards, all in excess of $100 or so.

But take heart. Unlike his superstar contemporaries in other sports, Aikman cards are exceedingly affordable. His Score Rookie Card books in the neighborhood of $45, a bargain compared to a Michael Jordan, Mickey Mantle, Wayne Gretzky or Ken Griffey Jr. RC. And it's easy to find common cards for $3 or less from virtually every year

of his career.

Aikman's primary link to the trading card industry comes through his role as corporate spokesman for the Score Board Inc., which owns Classic Games. Score Board owns Aikman's exclusive autographed memorabilia rights (under a three-year contract that is in the process of being renewed) and his exclusive autograph rights other than his numerous charitable functions and

**In the '90s, pogs have become popular collectibles — especially ones featuring Aikman.**

the occasional hobby show appearance.

"We saw Troy three years ago as the next great quarterback as the Cowboys were en route to their first Super Bowl," says Michael Balser, vice president of licensing for Score Board. "We probably finalized the deal around November 1993, and we did a longer deal with Troy than the average deal because we saw great things from him and believed the Cowboys were going to be a great team for a long time."

In addition to Classic cards, Score Board has produced almost 30 items autographed by Aikman in the last three years, ranging from a ceramic trading card with a wholesale price of $6, to pennants, plaques, photos and an autographed jersey with a hefty wholesale ticket of $400. All, Balser says, have sold out.

"We are constantly on back order for Aikman items," Balser says. "He doesn't sign a tremendous number of items for us, which is why it's so tough to get them. But he is one of our most popular athletes across

# HOBBY

Sports card manufacturers credit Troy Aikman's presence in the NFL as one of the reasons for the hobby's dramatic upswing

Somewhere in the bowels of a nearby trading card company, the midnight oil is burning. A team of functionaries, armed with a thesaurus, is feverishly trying to come up with new chase-card concepts that feature Troy Aikman.

Just think of the possibilities. Outstanding Okies? Bombshell Blondes? Three-Ring Masters? Country Boy Cuties?

Whatever theme is chosen, you can be assured that if manufacturers slap Aikman's picture on cardboard, it will sell. Big time.

It's no coincidence that Aikman's rookie season of 1989 coincides with the dawn of the modern era of football trading cards. Aikman is one of the key figures who has made the inaugural Score set from that year one of the most highly sought in the industry. Manufacturers have taken notice.

The running total is irrelevant, since manufacturers are coming up with new Aikman cards even as you read this sentence. But, for the record, as of April Fool's Day, 1996, he had appeared on an astounding 654 cards since those initial appearances in 1989.

No fooling.

What is even more staggering is the geometric progression of his popularity — three cards in 1989, 18 in 1990, 39 in 1991, 63 in 1992, 111 in 1993, 172 in 1994 and 251 in 1995. Certainly it is no coincidence that as Aikman has grown in stature, so has the football card industry.

"If he isn't the top guy, he's definitely in the top five," says Fleer/SkyBox spokesman Rich Bradley. "He has everything going for him that collectors look for. He plays the highest-profile position on the highest-profile team, and winning the Super Bowl certainly hasn't hurt his popularity.

"It's not true that we're planning a 450-card Troy Aikman set, but when a player is so popular, you do everything you can to include him in insert sets. There is not a chance of overexposure where Troy Aikman is concerned."

Should you wish to overexpose yourself, at least financially, it would cost you somewhere in the neighborhood of, say, $13,500 to buy every one of those 600-plus Aikman cards on the market. *(Please see the comprehensive checklist and Price Guide on page 102.)*

Top-dollar items: a 1995 ProLine

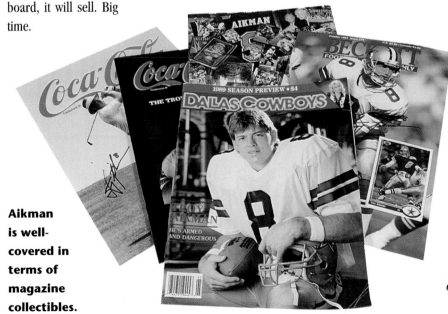

**Aikman is well-covered in terms of magazine collectibles.**

• 99 •
TROY AIKMAN

**Facial features lacking, Aikman still is an easily recognizable Kenner Starting Lineup figure.**

I don't think he has an exceptional appeal other than by the force of his talent."

One element of Aikman's marketing success, however, has been his appeal to women. Although the trading card field remains primarily a male domain, Score Board is branching out this year with an Aikman Christmas tree ornament. Designed by Hallmark, the ornament will be targeted toward women.

Sales projections, Balser says, are "extremely promising."

Mark Jordan, who presides over one of the nation's top memorabilia businesses from his office at The Ballpark in Arlington, ranks Aikman among the top five personalities in any sport in large part because of his appeal to women.

"You probably see more women wanting his things than

any guy right now," he says. "Anything with his photo sells to women. Your normal collector probably wants a ball or a helmet. Since he doesn't go around signing millions of things and since there is no shortage of Troy Aikman fans, anything sells."

Other than his contract with Score Board, Aikman is "pretty sedate when it comes to marketing his public personality," Jordan says. "He's not a 'Here I am, world,' kind of guy."

Aikman signs autographs frequently

the board."

One of the most remarkable elements of Aikman's popularity is that it has been achieved while playing on the same team as another of the game's top five personalities, running back Emmitt Smith.

And he hasn't gotten where he is, says Dallas card dealer Wayne Grove, just because he's cute.

"He does have that All-American boy persona, which is a lot of it, but he's a winner," Grove says. "He's not a pretty boy, though. I even have women who come in here who think he's ugly.

**The Breakfast of Champions honored Aikman and the Cowboys after their Super Bowl XXX triumph.**

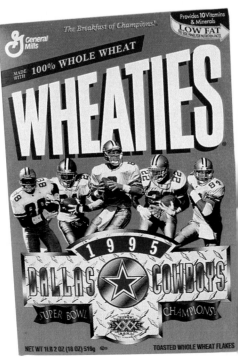

**Even the most hard-headed Cowboys fan would enjoy this collectible.**

in public, unlike many superstars, but infrequently ventures into the realm of autograph shows. However, he was the featured guest in February at a Phoenix show sponsored by Tri-Star Productions of Houston. Aikman autographs were a sellout, says Tri-Star's Jeff Rosenberg, even at $79 for flat items and $99 for helmets and jerseys.

"He was so cordial to everyone," Rosenberg says. "He seemed to be a real easygoing, laid-back guy who appreciates the adulation that comes to him. We had a large female contingent, more so than at our other shows, but then, kids love him, too. He appeals to everyone."

From the callow rookie who blew into Texas out of UCLA in 1989, Aikman has blossomed into a multimillion-dollar performer both on the field and off. He is one of the co-founders of the Quarterback Club, which represents the NFL's 30 most marketable stars. While no figures are available for retail sales of QB Club-licensed goods, consider the

fact that licensing revenues from the project topped $100 million last year, reports Colin Hagen of NFL Properties.

"There are not enough accolades I can give for Troy Aikman," Hagen says. "No higher praise can be bestowed upon him. He's immensely popular not only in Texas and the South, but nationally. He is one of those people who can transcend everything from the licensing end into the corporate sponsorships and anything else you want to mention.

"He has done this by being himself," Hagen continues. "The game of football is the quintessential team sport. You won't see players succeed by being bigger than the team. By Troy being who he is, he has elevated himself and his team and the game."

A game — and a hobby — that has become better off for knowing him. •

*David Barron writes a collectibles column for the* Houston Chronicle.

## SWIFT SALES

The following is a sampling of autographed Troy Aikman memorabilia items on the market:

| | |
|---|---|
| Replica jersey | $175 |
| Apex authentic jersey | $400 |
| Authentic football | $150 |
| Authentic helmet | $229 |
| Mini helmet | $119 |
| Numbered card | $35 |
| *Sports Illustrated* issue framed | $79 |

Source: Score Board/Classic catalog

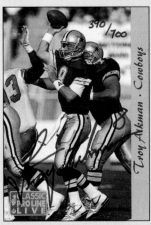

**1993 ProLine Live Autograph #51**

# A I K M A N

## Troy Aikman Comprehensive Card Checklist and Price Guide

❏ '89 Pro Set #490 $5
❏ '89 Score #270 $40
❏ '89 Topps Traded #70T
$2.50
❏ '90 Action Packed #51 $4
❏ '90 Action Packed
All-Madden #21 $2.50
❏ '90 FACT Pro Set Cincinnati
#78 $20
❏ '90 Fleer #384 $1.25
❏ '90 Kenner Starting
Lineup #1 $40
❏ '90 Little Big Leaguers #1
$6
❏ '90 Panini Stickers #240
$1.25
❏ '90 Pro Set #78 $1.25
❏ '90 Pro Set Collect-A-Books
#17 $.75
❏ '90 Score #21 $1.25
❏ '90 Score 100 Hottest
#14 $1.25
❏ '90 Score Young Superstars
#8 $1.50
❏ '90 Topps #3
Record Breaker $.60
❏ '90 Topps #482 $1.25
❏ '90 Topps #511
Team Leader $.50
❏ '90 Topps Tiffany #3
Record Breaker $3
❏ '90 Topps Tiffany #482
$6
❏ '90 Topps Tiffany #511
Team Leader $2.50
❏ '90-91 ProLine
Samples #3 $25
❏ '91 Action Packed #51
$2.50
❏ '91 Action Packed 24K
Gold #12G $100
❏ '91 All World Troy Aikman
Promo set (6) $20
❏ '91 Bowman #113
$1
❏ '91 Domino's Quarterbacks
#47 w/Staubach $.75
❏ '91 Domino's
Quarterbacks #6 $.75
❏ '91 FACT Pro Set
Mobil #128 $12
❏ '91 Fleer #228 $1
❏ '91 Fleer Stars'n'Stripes
#69 $1.25
❏ '91 Kenner Starting Lineup
#1 $55
❏ '91 Pacific #93 $1

❏ '91 Pacific Prototypes
#232 $60
❏ '91 Pinnacle #383
w/Staubach $1.50
❏ '91 Pinnacle #6 $5
❏ '91 Pro Set #128 $1
❏ '91 Pro Set #372A
Play it Straight $.60
❏ '91 Pro Set #372B
Play it Straight $.60
❏ '91 Pro Set Platinum #24
$1
❏ '91 Pro Set Police Dallas
#372 Play it Straight
$6
❏ '91 Pro Set Spanish #46
$.75
❏ '91 Pro Set UK Sheets #1
$12
❏ '91 ProLine Portraits #194
$1
❏ '91 ProLine Portraits
Autographs #194 $125
❏ '91 ProLine Punt Pass
and Kick #PPK1 $20
❏ '91 Score #225 $1
❏ '91 Score #631 MVP
$.50
❏ '91 Stadium Club #228
$6
❏ '91 Stadium Club
#299 F.J.Nunn's card
w/E.Smith $.50
❏ '91 Stadium Club SB
26 Logo #228 $30
❏ '91 Stadium Club SB 26
Logo #299 F.J.Nunn's card
w/E.Smith $2.50

**'89 Pro Set #490**

❏ '91 Star Pics #50 Flashback
$.35
❏ '91 Star Pics Auto. #50
Flashback $140
❏ '91 Topps #371 $1
❏ '91 Ultra #162 $1
❏ '91 Upper Deck #152 $1
❏ '91 Upper Deck #82
Team Checklist $.50
❏ '91 Wild Card * #68 $1
❏ '91 Wild Card NFL
Prototypes #1 $3.50
❏ '92 Action Packed
All-Madden #7 $2
❏ '92 Action Packed
All-Madden 24K Gold #7
$100
❏ '92 Action Packed Rookie
Update #76 $2.50
❏ '92 Action Packed Rookie
Update Gold Mint #76 $500
❏ '92 Action Packed Rookies
24K Gold #29G $100
❏ '92 All World #10
Legends in the Making $.50
❏ '92 All World #130 $1
❏ '92 All World Greats/
Rookies #SG1 $3
❏ '92 All World Legends/
Rookies #L10 $6
❏ '92 Breyers Bookmarks
#55 $10
❏ '92 Collector's Edge #31 $4
❏ '92 Diamond Stickers
#97 $.75
❏ '92 Dog Tags #40 $5
❏ '92 FACT NFL Properties
#3 $6
❏ '92 GameDay #227
$2.50
❏ '92 GameDay National #6
$6
❏ '92 Kenner Starting
Lineup #1 $30
❏ '92 Power #8 $1
❏ '92 Pro Set #401
Pro Bowl $.50
❏ '92 Pro Set #473 $1
❏ '92 ProLine Portraits
QB Gold #1 $1.50
❏ '92 ProLine Profiles
#181 $.50
❏ '92 ProLine Profiles
#182 $.50
❏ '92 ProLine Profiles
#183 $.50
❏ '92 ProLine Profiles

**'91 ProLine #194**

#184 $.50
❏ '92 ProLine Profiles
#185 $.50
❏ '92 ProLine Profiles
#186 $.50
❏ '92 ProLine Profiles
#187 $.50
❏ '92 ProLine Profiles
#188 $.50
❏ '92 ProLine Profiles
#189 $.50
❏ '92 ProLine Profiles
Autographs #181 $40
❏ '92 ProLine Profiles
Autographs #182 $40
❏ '92 ProLine Profiles
Autographs #183 $40
❏ '92 ProLine Profiles
Autographs #184 $40
❏ '92 ProLine Profiles
Autographs #185 $40
❏ '92 ProLine Profiles
Autographs #186 $40
❏ '92 ProLine Profiles
Autographs #187 $40
❏ '92 ProLine Profiles
Autographs #188 $40
❏ '92 ProLine Profiles
Autographs #189 $40
❏ '92 Quarterback
Greats GE #1 $3.50
❏ '92 SkyBox Impact #232 $1
❏ '92 SkyBox Impact
Major Impact #M11 $3
❏ '92 SkyBox Primetime
#313 Poster Card $1.25
❏ '92 SkyBox Primetime #8 $3
❏ '92 SkyBox Primetime

Poster Cards #M14 $10
❏ '92 Sport Decks #1C $.50
❏ '92 Stadium Club #602
Members Choice $4
❏ '92 Stadium Club #695 $8
❏ '92 Topps #744 $1
❏ '92 Topps Gold #744 $3
❏ '92 Upper Deck #597 $1
❏ '92 Upper Deck
Fanimation #F5 $6
❏ '92 Upper Deck Gold #G22
Quarterback Club $1
❏ '92 Upper Deck Gold
#G40 $1
❏ '92 Wild Card Field Force *
#11 $2.50
❏ '92 Wild Card Field Force
Gold #11 $10
❏ '92 Wild Card Field
Force Silver #11 $5
❏ '92 Wild Card Stat
Smashers * #SS17 $6
❏ '92-93 GameDay SB
Program #1 $5
❏ '92-93 Intimidator
Bio Sheets #1 $8
❏ '92-93 Pro Set Super Bowl
XXVII #20 $3
❏ '92-93 Upper Deck
NFL Experience #34 $1.50
❏ '92-93 Upper Deck NFL
Experience Gold #34 $7.50
❏ '93 Action Packed #11 $3
❏ '93 Action Packed 24K
Gold #1G $80
❏ '93 Action Packed ABC
MNF #61 $1.75
❏ '93 Action Packed ABC
MNF 24K Gold #61 $150
❏ '93 Action Packed
All-Madden #1 $1.75
❏ '93 Action Packed
All-Madden 24K Gold
#1G $60
❏ '93 Action Packed
All-Madden Prototype #1 $6
❏ '93 Action Packed QB Club
#QB1 $4
❏ '93 Action Packed QB
Club 24K Gold #QB1 $100
❏ '93 Action Packed QB
Club Braille #QB1B $12
❏ '93 Action Packed QB
Club Gold Mint #QB1 $500
❏ '93 Action Packed Rookies
Previews #RU1 $3
❏ '93 Action Packed Troy

Aikman Promos #TA2 $25
❏ '93 Action Packed Troy
Aikman Promos #TA3 $25
❏ '93 Bowman #1 Foil $6
❏ '93 Classic Draft #AU0
Auto. card; 1,000 signed
$175
❏ '93 Classic McDonald's
Four-Sport #1 $2.50
❏ '93 Classic Superhero
Comic #SS1 $20
❏ '93 Classic TONX #1 $.75
❏ '93 Collector's Edge #44 $1
❏ '93 Collector's Edge
Rookies FX #12 $2.50
❏ '93 Collector's Edge
Rookies FX Gold #12 $20
❏ '93 Dog Tags #49 $4
❏ '93 FACT Fleer Shell #66
$3.50
❏ '93 Fleer #253 Award
Winner $.50
❏ '93 Fleer #273 $1
❏ '93 Fleer Fruit of the
Loom #18 $10
❏ '93 GameDay #1 $2.50
❏ '93 GameDay
Gamebreakers #1 $5
❏ '93 Heads and Tails
SB XXVII #21 $1.50
❏ '93 Kenner Starting
Lineup #1 $20
❏ '93 McDonald's GameDay
All-Stars sheet A $2
❏ '93 McDonald's GameDay
Cowboys sheet A $2
❏ '93 Pacific #2 $1
❏ '93 Pacific Gold Prism

**'90 Action Packed #51**

Inserts #1 $25
❏ '93 Pacific Prisms #18 $8
❏ '93 Pacific Silver Prism
Inserts #1 $8
❏ '93 Pacific Silver Prism
Inserts Circular #1 $8
❏ '93 Pacific Triple Folder
Rookies/Superstars #1 $2.50
❏ '93 Pinnacle #281 $2.50
❏ '93 Pinnacle Team
Pinnacle w/Montana
#125 $1
❏ '93 Playoff #1 $4
❏ '93 Playoff #283 Playoff
Connections $2
❏ '93 Playoff Contenders
#25 $2.50
❏ '93 Power #8 $1
❏ '93 Power Gold #8 $2.50
❏ '93 Power Update Combos
#PC8 w/E.Smith $5
❏ '93 Power Update Combos
Gold #PC8 w/E.Smith
$7.50
❏ '93 Power Update Combos
Prisms #PC8 w/E.Smith
$12.50
❏ '93 Pro Set #25 Replay $.50
❏ '93 Pro Set #30 $1
❏ '93 ProLine Live #51 $1
❏ '93 ProLine Live Autographs
#51 Auto. card; 700 signed
$75
❏ '93 ProLine Live Illustrated
#SP1 $6
❏ '93 ProLine Live LPs #LP9 $5
❏ '93 ProLine Live Promo
#51 $5
❏ '93 ProLine Live Tonx #1 $2
❏ '93 ProLine Previews
#PL1 $20
❏ '93 Rice Council * #2 $3
❏ '93 Score #238 $1
❏ '93 Score #411 Super
Bowl $.50
❏ '93 Score Ore-Ida QB
Club #10 $3.50
❏ '93 Select #7 $6
❏ '93 Select Gridiron Skills
#5 $75
❏ '93 Select Young Stars
#13 $10
❏ '93 SkyBox #10 $2.50
❏ '93 SkyBox Impact #66 $1
❏ '93 SkyBox Impact Colors
#66 $4
❏ '93 SkyBox Poster Cards

**'92 All World #10**
**Legends in the Making**

#2 w/Irvin/E.Smith/
Maryland $.30
❏ '93 SkyBox Thunder and
Lightning #6 w/Irvin $10
❏ '93 SP #64 $10
❏ '93 SP All-Pros #3 $80
❏ '93 Spectrum QB Club
Tribute Sheet Promo #1 $4
❏ '93 Spectrum QB Club
Tribute Sheets #1 $4
❏ '93 Stadium Club #242
Members Choice $1.25
❏ '93 Stadium Club #50 $2.50
❏ '93 Stadium Club Division
Winner #50 $5
❏ '93 Stadium Club First
Day Issue #242 Members
Choice $40
❏ '93 Stadium Club First
Day Issue #50 $75
❏ '93 Stadium Club NFC
Champ. Master Photos
#1 $5
❏ '93 Stadium Club Super
Team Redemption #242
Members Choice $4
❏ '93 Stadium Club Super
Team Redemption #50 7.50
❏ '93 Topps 530 $1
❏ '93 Topps Black Gold #8 $5
❏ '93 Topps FantaSports #6
$7.50
❏ '93 Topps Gold #530 $4
❏ '93 U.S. Playing Cards
Ditka's Picks #1S $.50
❏ '93 Ultra #85 $3.50
❏ '93 Ultra Award

Winners #1 $30

❑ '93 Upper Deck #140 $1

❑ '93 Upper Deck America's Team #AT14 Checklist $12

❑ '93 Upper Deck America's Team #AT8 $30

❑ '93 Upper Deck America's Team Jumbos #AT14 Checklist $6

❑ '93 Upper Deck America's Team Jumbos #AT8 $15

❑ '93 Upper Deck Future Heroes #40 $4

❑ '93 Upper Deck Pro Bowl #PB13 $25

❑ '93 Upper Deck Team Cowboys #D23 $1.75

❑ '93 Upper Deck Team Cowboys #D25 $1

❑ '93 Upper Deck Team MVPs #TM11 $4

❑ '93 Wild Card * #86 $1

❑ '93 Wild Card Field Force * #70 $2

❑ '93 Wild Card Field Force Gold #70 $3.50

❑ '93 Wild Card Field Force Silver #70 $2.50

❑ '93 Wild Card Field Force Superchrome #5 $2

❑ '93 Wild Card Stat Smashers * #79 $4

❑ '93 Wild Card Stat Smashers Gold #79 $5

❑ '93 Wild Card Superchrome #86 $3

❑ '93 Wild Card Superchrome FF/RHR B/B #1 w/ Stubblefield $3

❑ '93-94 Bleachers Troy Aikman Promo set (4) $10

❑ '93-94 Upper Deck Miller Lite SB #1 w/Kelly $5

❑ '93-95 NFL Properties Show Redemption #5 $15

❑ '94 Action Packed #120 Super Bowl $3

❑ '94 Action Packed

**'93 SP All-Pro #AP3**

#172 Quarterback Club $1.50

❑ '94 Action Packed #20 $3

❑ '94 Action Packed 24K Gold #1G $75

❑ '94 Action Packed 24K Gold #43G Quarterback Club $60

❑ '94 Action Packed 24K Prototypes #MMP2G $30

❑ '94 Action Packed All-Madden #29 $1.50

❑ '94 Action Packed All-Madden 24K Gold #29G $90

❑ '94 Action Packed Braille #120 Super Bowl $6

❑ '94 Action Packed Braille #172 Quarterback Club $3

❑ '94 Action Packed Braille #20 $6

❑ '94 Action Packed CoaStars #1 $2.50

❑ '94 Action Packed Fantasy Forecast #5 $2.50

❑ '94 Action Packed Gold Signature #120 Super Bowl $7.50

❑ '94 Action Packed Gold Signature #172 Quarterback Club $4

❑ '94 Action Packed Gold Signature #20 $7.50

❑ '94 Action Packed Mammoth #MM1 $7

❑ '94 Action Packed Mammoth Prototype#MMP0 $10

❑ '94 Action Packed Monday Night FB Silver #11S $75

❑ '94 Action Packed Monday Night FB Sterling Silver #11S $500

❑ '94 Action Packed Monday Night Football #54 $1.50

❑ '94 Action Packed Prototypes #FB941 $7

❑ '94 Action Packed Quarterback Challenge #FA3 $2.50

❑ '94 Action Packed Quarterback Club #1 $3

❑ '94 Bleachers 23K Troy Aikman set (3) $20

❑ '94 Bowman #95 $3

❑ '94 Classic Draft #96 Flashback $.30

❑ '94 Classic Draft Gold #96 Flashback $1

❑ '94 Classic International Promos #1 $5

❑ '94 Classic NFL Experience #21 $1

❑ '94 Classic NFL Experience #SP1 $70

❑ '94 Classic NFL Experience Promos #1 $6

❑ '94 Collector's Choice

**'93 Select Gridiron Skills #5**

#342 $1

❑ '94 Collector's Choice Crash the Game #C2 Blue $4

❑ '94 Collector's Choice Crash the Game #C2 Green $4

❑ '94 Collector's Choice Crash the Game #C2 Gold Winner $2

❑ '94 Collector's Choice Crash the Game #C2 Silver Winner $1.25

❑ '94 Collector's Choice Crash the Game #C2 Bronze Winner $.75

❑ '94 Collector's Choice Gold #342 $50

❑ '94 Collector's Choice Silver #342 $4

❑ '94 Collector's Edge #41 $1.25

❑ '94 Collector's Edge Boss Squad #6 $4

❑ '94 Collector's Edge Boss Squad Bronze EQII #6 $4

❑ '94 Collector's Edge Boss Squad Gold Helmet #6 $4

❑ '94 Collector's Edge Boss Squad Silver #6 $4

❑ '94 Collector's Edge FX #3 $8

❑ '94 Collector's Edge FX Gold Back #3 $40

❑ '94 Collector's Edge FX Gold Letters #3 $25

❑ '94 Collector's Edge FX Gold Shield #3 $40

❑ '94 Collector's Edge FX Red Letters #3 $4

❑ '94 Collector's Edge FX Silver Back #3 $6

❑ '94 Collector's Edge FX Silver Letters #3 $6

❑ '94 Collector's Edge FX

Silver Shield #3 $40

❑ '94 Collector's Edge FX White Back #3 $6

❑ '94 Collector's Edge Gold #41 $3

❑ '94 Collector's Edge Pop Warner #41 $2.50

❑ '94 Collector's Edge Pop Warner Gold #41 $10

❑ '94 Collector's Edge Silver #41 $2.50

❑ '94 Costacos Brothers Poster Cards #1 $1.50

❑ '94 Cowboys ProLine Live Kroger Stickers #1 w/Woodson/E.Williams $1.25

❑ '94 Excalibur #12 $3.50

❑ '94 Excalibur 22K Gold #1 $8

❑ '94 Excalibur FX #7 $8

❑ '94 Excalibur FX Gold Shield EQ #7 $10

❑ '94 Excalibur FX Gold Shield FX #7 $30

❑ '94 Excalibur FX Silver Shield EQ #7 $6

❑ '94 FACT Fleer Shell #95 $1.50

❑ '94 FACT NFL Properties #1 $3.50

❑ '94 FACT NFL Properties Artex #1 $1.25

❑ '94 Finest #202 $10

❑ '94 Finest Refractors #202 75

❑ '94 Fleer #107 $1

❑ '94 Fleer All-Pros #1 $3

❑ '94 Fleer Pro-Visions #5 $1.50

❑ '94 GameDay #91 $2

❑ '94 GameDay Gamebreakers #1 $3

❑ '94 Images #105 $3

❑ '94 Images All-Pro #A4 $30

❑ '94 Kenner Starting Lineup #1 $18

❑ '94 Pacific #1 $1

❑ '94 Pacific Gems of the Crown #1 $12

❑ '94 Pacific Marquee Prisms #1 $3

❑ '94 Pacific Marquee Prisms Gold #1 $20

❑ '94 Pacific Prisms #1 $10

❑ '94 Pacific Prisms Gold #1 $50

❑ '94 Pacific Triple Folders #7 $1.75

❑ '94 Pacific Triple Folders Rookies/Superstars #8 $1.50

❑ '94 Pinnacle #150 $2

❑ '94 Pinnacle Canton Bound #1 $1.50

❑ '94 Pinnacle Performers #PP1 $10

❑ '94 Pinnacle Team

Pinnacle #TP1
w/Montana                    $80
❏ '94 Pinnacle Trophy
Collection #150              $50
❏ '94 Playoff #25             $3
❏ '94 Playoff #263
Super Bowl                  $1.25
❏ '94 Playoff Contenders
#45                         $3.50
❏ '94 Playoff Contenders
Back-to-Back
w/S.Young #175              $5
❏ '94 Playoff Contenders
Throwbacks #7               $30
❏ '94 Playoff Super Bowl
Redemption #1               $12
❏ '94 Pro Mags #26           $3
❏ '94 Pro Mags Promos *
#2                          $3.50
❏ '94 Pro Tags #37            $3
❏ '94 ProLine Live #26        $1
❏ '94 ProLine Live #390
w/Irvin                     $.60
❏ '94 ProLine Live
Autographs #26 Auto.
card; 340 signed           $175
❏ '94 ProLine Live
Autographs #390 Auto.
card w/Irvin; 345 signed
                           $250
❏ '94 ProLine Live Draft
Day Prototypes #FD6          $3
❏ '94 ProLine Live MVP
Sweepstakes #5              $25
❏ '94 ProLine Live Previews
#PL1                        $12
❏ '94 ProLine Live Spotlight
#PB4                         $2
❏ '94 Score #2              $.75
❏ '94 Score Board National
Promos #10                   $3
❏ '94 Score Board Nationa
Promos #20A Checklist        $6
❏ '94 Score Dream Team
#1                          $30
❏ '94 Score Gold #2          $4

❏ '94 Select #40            $3.50
❏ '94 Select Canton
Bound #CB11                 $50
❏ '94 SkyBox #37             $3
❏ '94 SkyBox Impact #57      $1
❏ '94 SkyBox Impact
Ultimate Impact #U1         $10
❏ '94 SkyBox Revolution
#R3                         $20
❏ '94 SkyBox SkyTech
Stars #ST1                   $8
❏ '94 SP #117                $4
❏ '94 SP All-Pro Holoview
Die Cuts #PB9              $180
❏ '94 SP All-Pro Holoviews
#PB9                        $18
❏ '94 SP Die Cuts #117      $12
❏ '94 Sportflics #178
Starflics                   $1.50
❏ '94 Sportflics #31        $2.50
❏ '94 Sportflics Artist's
Proofs #178 Starflics       $25
❏ '94 Sportflics Artist's
Proofs #31                  $45
❏ '94 Sportflics Head-
To-Head #HH6
w/R.White                   $25
❏ '94 Stadium Club
#520 Red Zone                $1
❏ '94 Stadium Club #540      $2
❏ '94 Stadium Club
#590                        $1.50
❏ '94 Stadium Club
Bowman's Best #22
w/Shuler                     $7
❏ '94 Stadium Club
Bowman's Best #BK13          $7
❏ '94 Stadium Club
Bowman's Best Refractors
#22 w/Shuler                $35
❏ '94 Stadium Club
Bowman's Best Refractors
#BK13                       $30
❏ '94 Stadium Club
Division Winner #540         $4
❏ '94 Stadium Club
Dynasty and Destiny #4
w/Fouts                      $7
❏ '94 Stadium Club First Day
Issue #520 Red Zone         $25
❏ '94 Stadium Club
First Day Issue #540        $50
❏ '94 Stadium Club
First Day Issue #590        $40
❏ '94 Stadium Club
Super Team Redemption
#520 Red Zone                $2
❏ '94 Stadium Club Super
Team Redemption #540         $4
❏ '94 Stadium Club Super
Team Redemption #590         $3
❏ '94 Topps #200 Tools
of the Game                $.50
❏ '94 Topps #316  Measure
of Greatness               $.50
❏ '94 Topps #400             $1
❏ '94 Topps #1,000

**'94 Stadium Club #590**

/3,000                      $30
❏ '94 Topps All-Pro #9      $10
❏ '94 Topps Special
Effects #200 Tools of
the Game                     $4
❏ '94 Topps Special Effects
#316 Measure of
Greatness                    $4
❏ '94 Topps Special Effects
#400                         $8
❏ '94 U.S. Playing Cards
Ditka's Picks #11C         $.50
❏ '94 Ultra #67              $2
❏ '94 Ultra Flair Hot
Numbers #1                   $3
❏ '94 Ultra Stars #1        $35
❏ '94 Upper Deck #277       $1.50
❏ '94 Upper Deck 24K
Gold #1                     $75
❏ '94 Upper Deck Electric
Gold #277                   $60
❏ '94 Upper Deck Electric
Silver #277                $7.50
❏ '94 Upper Deck Predictor
League Leaders #RP1          $5
❏ '94 Upper Deck Predictor
League Leaders Winner
#RP1                         $2
❏ '94-95 Classic Assets #3 $.60
❏ '94-95 Classic Assets
#28                        $.60
❏ '94-95 Classic Assets
Die Cuts #DC3                $7
❏ '94-95 Classic Assets
Phone Cards $100 #1        $160
❏ '94-95 Classic Assets
Phone Cards $25 #NNO
w/S.Young                   $60
❏ '94-95 Classic Assets
Phone Cards $5 #1           $12
❏ '94-95 Classic Assets
Phone Cards One
Minute/$2 #1                 $5
❏ '94-95 Classic Assets
Silver Signature #3        $3.50
❏ '94-95 Images Update
#12                        $127
❏ '95 Action Packed #20      $2

❏ '95 Action Packed 24K
Gold #12G                   $70
❏ '95 Action Packed ABC
MNF Promos #3A             $2.50
❏ '95 Action Packed Armed
Forces #3                   $15
❏ '95 Action Packed Armed
Forces Braille #3           $30
❏ '95 Action Packed MNF
24K Gold Team #7            $45
❏ '95 Action Packed MNF
Highlights #107 Classic      $6
❏ '95 Action Packed MNF
Highlights #3               $15
❏ '95 Action Packed MNF
Night Flight #4             $12
❏ '95 Action Packed
Monday Night Football
#107 Classic               $.60
❏ '95 Action Packed
Monday Night Football
#3                         $1.50
❏ '95 Action Packed
Quicksilver #20             $30
❏ '95 Action Packed
Rocket Men #11              $16
❏ '95 Action Packed
Rookies/Stars #38          $1.50
❏ '95 Action Packed
Rookies/Stars 24K
Gold Team #7                $50
❏ '95 Action Packed
Rookies/Stars Closing
Seconds #8                  $15
❏ '95 Action Packed
Rookies/Stars Stargazers
#38                         $18
❏ '95 Bowman #198          $1.50
❏ '95 Bowman's Best #V8      $6
❏ '95 Bowman's Best
Refractors #V8              $60
❏ '95 Classic NFL Experience
#25                        $.75
❏ '95 Classic NFL Experience
Gold #25                     $2
❏ '95 Classic NFL
Experience Super Bowl
Game #N0                     $2
❏ '95 Classic NFL Rookies
#109                       $.30
❏ '95 Classic NFL Rookies
Printer's Proofs #109       $15
❏ '95 Classic NFL Rookies
Silver #109                  $2
❏ '95 Classic NFL Rookies
Silver Printer's Proofs
#109                        $30
❏ '95 Cleo Quarterback
Club Valentines #1         $.50
❏ '95 Collector's Choice
#66                          $1
❏ '95 Collector's Choice
Crash The Game #C7A
9/4                        $1.25
❏ '95 Collector's Choice
Crash The Game #C7B
10/1                       $1.25

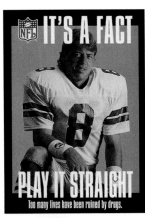

**'94 FACT NFL
Properties #1**

❏ '95 Collector's Choice Crash The Game #C7C 11/12 $1.25
❏ '95 Collector's Choice Crash The Game Gold #C7A 9/4 $4
❏ '95 Collector's Choice Crash The Game Gold #C7B 10/1 $4
❏ '95 Collector's Choice Crash The Game Gold #C7C 11/12 $4
❏ '95 Collector's Choice CTG Gold Red. #C7 $2.50
❏ '95 Collector's Choice CTG Gold TD Red. #C7 $7.50
❏ '95 Collector's Choice CTG Silver Red. #C7 $.60
❏ '95 Collector's Choice CTG Silver TD Red. #C7 $2.50
❏ '95 Collector's Choice Players Club #66 $2.50
❏ '95 Collector's Choice Players Club Platinum #66 $30
❏ '95 Collector's Choice Upd. #U64 The Key $.50
❏ '95 Collector's Choice Upd. Crash the Playoffs #CP4 $2.50
❏ '95 Collector's Choice Upd. Crash the Playoffs Gold #CP4 $7.50
❏ '95 Collector's Choice Upd. Gold #U64 The Key $15
❏ '95 Collector's Choice Upd. Silver #U64 The Key $1.50
❏ '95 Collector's Choice Upd. Stick-Ums #51 /Sherrard/Barnett/Krieg $.30
❏ '95 Collector's Edge #50 $1
❏ '95 Collector's Edge 22K Gold #50 $90
❏ '95 Collector's Edge

❏ '95 Collector's Edge Black Label #50 $1
❏ '95 Collector's Edge Black Label 22K Gold #50 $90
❏ '95 Collector's Edge Black Label Silver Die Cut #50 $16
❏ '95 Collector's Edge Die Cut #50 $8
❏ '95 Collector's Edge EdgeTech #20 $10
❏ '95 Collector's Edge EdgeTech 22K Gold #20 $30
❏ '95 Collector's Edge EdgeTech Black Label #20 $10
❏ '95 Collector's Edge EdgeTech Circular Prisms #20 $5
❏ '95 Collector's Edge EdgeTech Quantum #20 $50
❏ '95 Collector's Edge EdgeTech Quantum Die Cuts #20 $100
❏ '95 Collector's Edge Gold Logo #50 $1
❏ '95 Collector's Edge Instant Replay #6 $1
❏ '95 Collector's Edge Instant Replay Prism #6 $3
❏ '95 Collector's Edge TimeWarp #2 w/Marchetti $90
❏ '95 Collector's Edge TimeWarp 22K Gold #2 w/Marchetti $225
❏ '95 Collector's Edge TimeWarp Black Label #2 w/Marchetti $90
❏ '95 Collector's Edge Tim Warp Prisms #2 w/Marchetti $90
❏ '95 Excalibur #18 $3.50
❏ '95 Excalibur 22K Gold #8SW $70
❏ '95 Excalibur 22K Gold Prisms #8SW $250
❏ '95 Excalibur Die Cuts #18 $25
❏ '95 Excalibur Dragon Slayers #1 $7
❏ '95 Excalibur TekTech #1 $60
❏ '95 Finest #185 $7
❏ '95 Finest Fan Favorites #FF5 $25
❏ '95 Finest Refractors #185 $70
❏ '95 Flair #51 $3
❏ '95 Fleer #90 $1
❏ '95 Fleer Metal #48 $2
❏ '95 Fleer Metal Gold Blasters #1 $7
❏ '95 Fleer Metal Silver Flashers #1 $5
❏ '95 Images Limited #8 $2

'95 Fleer #90

'95 Pinnacle Showcase

❏ '95 Images Limited/Live Die Cuts #DC4 $30
❏ '95 Images Limited/Live Focused #F8 w/E.Smith $25
❏ '95 Images Limited/Live Icons #I4 $15
❏ '95 Images Limited/ Live Silks #S1 $75
❏ '95 Images Limited/Live Untouchables #U4 $15
❏ '95 Images Live #8 $2
❏ '95 Kenner Starting Lineup #1 $14
❏ '95 Pacific #37 $1
❏ '95 Pacific Blue #37 $6
❏ '95 Pacific Crown Royale #75 $6
❏ '95 Pacific Crown Royale Blue #75 $35
❏ '95 Pacific Crown Royale Copper #75 $30
❏ '95 Pacific Crown Royale Pride of the NFL #PN8 $20
❏ '95 Pacific Crown Royale Pro Bowl Die Cuts #PB11 $60
❏ '95 Pacific Gems of the Crown #GC8 $12
❏ '95 Pacific Gold Crown Die-Cuts #DC4 $30
❏ '95 Pacific Gold Crown Die-Cuts Flat Gold #DC4 $60
❏ '95 Pacific Gridiron Blue #33 $5
❏ '95 Pacific Gridiron Copper #33 $40
❏ '95 Pacific Gridiron Gold #33 $600
❏ '95 Pacific Gridiron Platinum #33 $40
❏ '95 Pacific Gridiron Red #33 $5
❏ '95 Pacific Hometown Heroes #HH2 $8
❏ '95 Pacific Platinum #37 $6
❏ '95 Pacific Prisms #19 $8

❏ '95 Pacific Prisms Connections #8A $40
❏ '95 Pacific Prisms Connections Blue #8A $120
❏ '95 Pacific Prisms Gold #19 $40
❏ '95 Pacific Triple Folders #46 $2
❏ '95 Pacific Triple Folders Careers #1 $50
❏ '95 Pacific Triple Folders Crystalline #1 $10
❏ '95 Pacific Triple Folders Rookies/Stars #7 $1.50
❏ '95 Pacific Triple Folders Rookies/Stars Blue #7 $7.50
❏ '95 Pacific Triple Folders Rookies/Stars Raspberry #7 $7.50
❏ '95 Pacific Triple Folders Teams #11 w/Irvin /E.Smith $5
❏ '95 Pinnacle #195 Pinnacle Passer $.75
❏ '95 Pinnacle #2 $1.50
❏ '95 Pinnacle Artist's Proof #195 Pinnacle Passer $40
❏ '95 Pinnacle Artist's Proof #2 $90
❏ '95 Pinnacle Clear Shots #8 $20
❏ '95 Pinnacle Club Collection #19 $.50
❏ '95 Pinnacle Club Collection #20 $.50
❏ '95 Pinnacle Club Collection #21 $.50
❏ '95 Pinnacle Club Collection #22 $.50
❏ '95 Pinnacle Club Collection #23 $.50
❏ '95 Pinnacle Club Collection #24 $.50
❏ '95 Pinnacle Club Collection #25 $.50
❏ '95 Pinnacle Club Collection #26 $.50
❏ '95 Pinnacle Club Collection #27 $.50
❏ '95 Pinnacle Club Collection Aerial Assault #1 $25
❏ '95 Pinnacle Club Collection Arms Race #2 $12
❏ '95 Pinnacle Gamebreakers #6 $18
❏ '95 Pinnacle Showcase #6 $12
❏ '95 Pinnacle Team Pinnacle #4 w/Marino $100
❏ '95 Pinnacle Trophy Collection #195 Pinnacle Passer $10
❏ '95 Pinnacle Trophy Collection #2 $20
❏ '95 Playoff Absolute #50 $2

- ❏ '95 Playoff Absolute Quad #2 w/Bledsoe /Favre/Mirer — $225
- ❏ '95 Playoff Contenders #8 — $2
- ❏ '95 Playoff Contenders Back-To-Back #1 w/Marino — $225
- ❏ '95 Playoff Contenders Hog Heaven #HH1 — $90
- ❏ '95 Playoff Prime #50 — $1
- ❏ '95 Playoff Prime Minis #50 — $40
- ❏ '95 ProLine #254 — $1
- ❏ '95 ProLine Autographs #254 Auto. card; 500 signed — $100
- ❏ '95 ProLine Bonus Card Jumbos #9 — $16
- ❏ '95 ProLine Game of the Week #H26 w/Mamula — $1.50
- ❏ '95 ProLine GameBreakers #GB1 — $12
- ❏ '95 ProLine GameBreakers Printer's Proofs #GB1 — $80
- ❏ '95 ProLine Impact #3 — $12
- ❏ '95 ProLine Impact Golden #3 — $35
- ❏ '95 ProLine MVP Redemption #9 — $16
- ❏ '95 ProLine MVP Redemption # out of 200 #9 — $65
- ❏ '95 ProLine National #254 — $5
- ❏ '95 ProLine Phone Cards 1.00 #4 — $3.50
- ❏ '95 ProLine Phone Cards 1.00 Artist's Proofs #4 — $14
- ❏ '95 ProLine Phone Cards 100.00 #5 — $160
- ❏ '95 ProLine Phone Cards 1,000.00 #4 — $1,800
- ❏ '95 ProLine Phone Cards 2.00 #4 — $7
- ❏ '95 ProLine Phone Cards

- 2.00 Artist's Proofs #4 — $25
- ❏ '95 ProLine Phone Cards 5.00 #2 — $14
- ❏ '95 ProLine Precision Cuts #P6 — $30
- ❏ '95 ProLine Previews Phone Cards 2.00 #1 — $10
- ❏ '95 ProLine Previews Phone Cards 5.00 #1 — $20
- ❏ '95 ProLine Printer's Proofs #254 — $35
- ❏ '95 ProLine Printer's Proofs Silver #254 — $70
- ❏ '95 ProLine Pro Bowl #PB5 — $2.50
- ❏ '95 ProLine Series II #12 — $1
- ❏ '95 ProLine Series II Printer's Proofs #12 — $18
- ❏ '95 ProLine Silver #254 — $4
- ❏ '95 Score #15 — $.75
- ❏ '95 Score #215 Star Struck — $.50
- ❏ '95 Score #236 Checklist — $.25
- ❏ '95 Score Dream Team #DT2 — $20
- ❏ '95 Score Offense Inc. #7 — $12
- ❏ '95 Score Pass Time #PT4 — $20
- ❏ '95 Score Promos #DT2 Dream Team — $5
- ❏ '95 Score Red Siege #15 — $7.50
- ❏ '95 Score Red Siege #215 Star Struck — $5
- ❏ '95 Score Red Siege #236 Checklist — $2.50
- ❏ '95 Score Red Siege Artist's Proofs #15 — $35
- ❏ '95 Score Red Siege Artist's Proofs #215 Star Struck — $25
- ❏ '95 Score Red Siege Artist's Proofs #236 Checklist — $12
- ❏ '95 Select Certified #44 — $4
- ❏ '95 Select Certified Checklists #5 — $.25
- ❏ '95 Select Certified Gold Team #5 — $60
- ❏ '95 Select Certified Mirror Gold #44 — $50
- ❏ '95 Select Certified Select Few 1028 #7 — $60
- ❏ '95 Select Certified Select Few 2250 #7 — $50
- ❏ '95 SkyBox #32 — $1.50
- ❏ '95 SkyBox Impact #34 — $.75
- ❏ '95 SkyBox Impact Countdown #C4 — $8
- ❏ '95 SkyBox Impact Future Hall of Famers #HF8 — $30
- ❏ '95 SkyBox Impact Power #IP27 — $4
- ❏ '95 SkyBox Paydirt #PD1 — $6

**'95 Zenith Second Season # 587**

- ❏ '95 SkyBox Paydirt Colors #PD1 — $.50
- ❏ '95 SP #39 — $4
- ❏ '95 SP All-Pros #8 — $7
- ❏ '95 SP All-Pros Gold #8 — $55
- ❏ '95 SP Championship #88 — $2
- ❏ '95 SP Championship Die Cuts #88 — $8
- ❏ '95 SP Championship Playoff Showcase #PS1 — $18
- ❏ '95 SP Championship Playoff Showcase Die Cuts #PS1 — $35
- ❏ '95 SP Holoviews #29 — $12
- ❏ '95 SP Holoviews Die Cuts #29 — $110
- ❏ '95 Sportflix #1 — $1.25
- ❏ '95 Sportflix #154 Game Winners — $.60
- ❏ '95 Sportflix Artist's Proofs #1 — $35
- ❏ '95 Sportflix Artist's Proofs #154 Game Winners — $18
- ❏ '95 Sportflix Man 2 Man #1 w/Marino — $20
- ❏ '95 Sportflix ProMotion #2 — $20
- ❏ '95 Stadium Club #188 Extreme Corps — $3
- ❏ '95 Stadium Club #300 — $1.50
- ❏ '95 Stadium Club Extreme Corps Diffractions #188 — $4
- ❏ '95 Stadium Club Nemeses #8 w/M.Brooks — $15
- ❏ '95 Stadium Club Nightmares #NM15 — $20
- ❏ '95 Summit #188 Offensive Weapons — $.75
- ❏ '95 Summit #198 Checklist — $.40
- ❏ '95 Summit #35 — $1.50
- ❏ '95 Summit Ground

- Zero #188 Offensive Weapons — $12
- ❏ '95 Summit Ground Zero #198 Checklist — $6
- ❏ '95 Summit Ground Zero #35 — $25
- ❏ '95 Summit Team Summit #4 — $50
- ❏ '95 Topps #130 — $1
- ❏ '95 Topps Air Raid #10 w/Irvin — $10
- ❏ '95 Topps Finest Boosters #B170 — $10
- ❏ '95 Topps Finest Boosters Refractors #B170 — $20
- ❏ '95 Topps Finest Inserts #1 — $12
- ❏ '95 Topps Finest Refractors #1 — $25
- ❏ '95 Topps Jaguars Inaugural #130 — $2
- ❏ '95 Topps Panthers Inaugural #130 — $2
- ❏ '95 Topps Profiles #15 — $6
- ❏ '95 Ultra #483 Extra Stars — $1
- ❏ '95 Ultra #71 — $1.50
- ❏ '95 Ultra Gold Medallion #483 Extra Stars — $6
- ❏ '95 Ultra Gold Medallion #71 — $9
- ❏ '95 Ultra Overdrive #2 — $10
- ❏ '95 Ultra Ultrabilities #5 — $5
- ❏ '95 Upper Deck #32 — $1.50
- ❏ '95 Upper Deck Electric Gold #32 — $50
- ❏ '95 Upper Deck Electric Silver #32 — $6
- ❏ '95 Upper Deck Predictor Award Winners #HP4 — $10
- ❏ '95 Upper Deck Predictor League Leaders #RP4 — $10
- ❏ '95 Upper Deck Pro Bowl #PB11 — $20
- ❏ '95 Upper Deck Special Edition #SE36 — $3.50
- ❏ '95 Upper Deck Special Edition Gold #SE36 — $30
- ❏ '95 Zenith #Z66 — $8
- ❏ '95 Zenith Second Season #SS7 — $12
- ❏ '95 Zenith Z-Team #ZT2 — $60
- ❏ 1996 Classic NFL Experience #8 — $.75
- ❏ '96 Classic NFL Experience Printer's Proofs #8 — $18
- ❏ '96 Classic NFL Experience Sculpted #S5 — $12
- ❏ '96 Classic NFL Experience Super Bowl Game #N3 — $3
- ❏ '96 SPX #11 — $10
- ❏ '96 SPX Gold #11 — $30
- ❏ '96 SPX Holofame #HM1 — $30

* Multiple stripe versions not listed

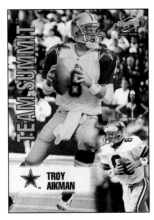

**'95 Summit Team Summit #4**

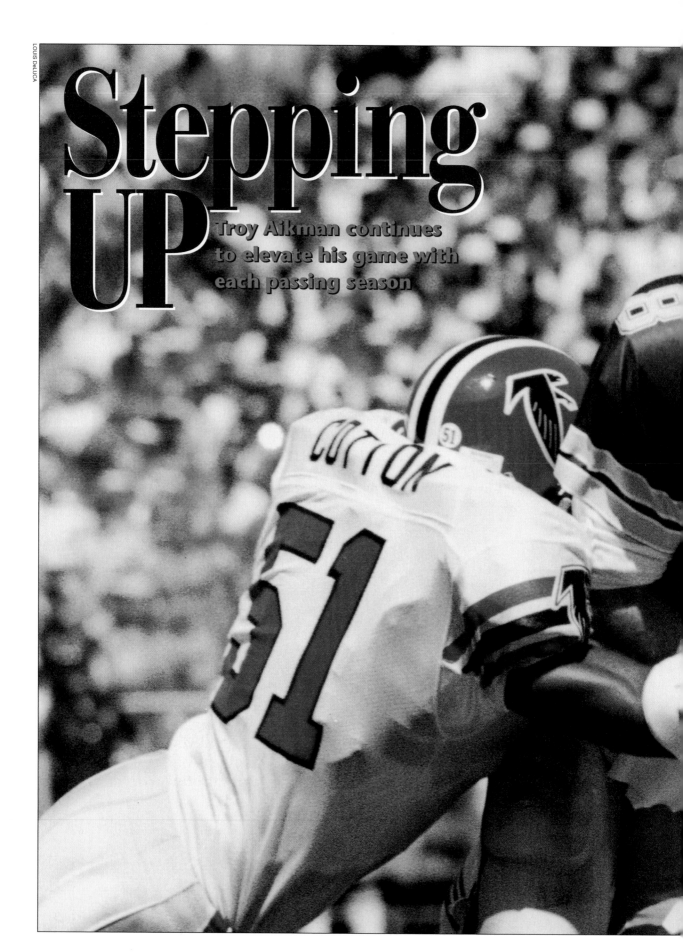

# Stepping UP

**Troy Aikman continues to elevate his game with each passing season**

# 1989

- Becomes first Cowboys rookie quarterback to start a season opener since Roger Staubach in 1969.
- Completes 17 of 35 passes for 180 yards in NFL debut Sept. 10 at New Orleans.
- Throws first career touchdown pass, Sept. 17 at Atlanta — a 65-yarder to Michael Irvin.
- Breaks left index finger early in the team's loss to the New York Giants and misses the following five games.
- Records an NFL rookie-record 379 yards passing at Phoenix in his first game back after the injury.
- Also at Phoenix, Aikman is knocked unconscious as he fires a 75-yard TD strike to James Dixon late in the fourth quarter to put Dallas ahead briefly.
- Throws for four touchdown passes during 35-31 loss to the Rams.
- Named to most All-Rookie teams.

**1989 [1-15; FIFTH PLACE, NFC EAST]**

|  | Att. | Comp. | Yds. | TD | Int. | Long |
|---|---|---|---|---|---|---|
| L-@ New Orleans 9/10 | 35 | 17 | 180 | 0 | 2 | 24 |
| L-@ Atlanta 9/17 | 23 | 13 | 241 | 1 | 2 | 65t |
| L- Washington 9/24 | 21 | 6 | 83 | 0 | 2 | 36 |
| L- N.Y. Giants 10/1 | 6 | 1 | 11 | 0 | 0 | 11 |
| L-@ Green Bay 10/8 | DNP - broken finger | | | | | |
| L- San Francisco 10/15 | DNP - broken finger | | | | | |
| L-@ Kansas City 10/22 | DNP - broken finger | | | | | |
| L- Phoenix 10/29 | DNP - broken finger | | | | | |
| W-@ Washington 11/5 | DNP - broken finger | | | | | |
| L-@ Phoenix 11/12 | 40 | 21 | 379 | 2 | 2 | 75t |
| L- Miami 11/19 | 33 | 25 | 261 | 1 | 1 | 21 |
| L- Philadelphia 11/23 | 21 | 7 | 54 | 0 | 3 | 13 |
| L- L.A. Rams 12/3 | 34 | 19 | 179 | 4 | 1 | 35t |
| L-@ Philadelphia 12/10 | 30 | 17 | 152 | 1 | 0 | 21 |
| L-@ N.Y. Giants 12/16 | 22 | 11 | 84 | 0 | 1 | 22 |
| L- Green Bay 12/24 | 28 | 18 | 125 | 0 | 4 | 21 |
| **Totals** | **293** | **155** | **1,749** | **9** | **18** | **75t** |

TROY AIKMAN

# 1990

- Claims first NFL victory as a starter with a 17-14 triumph over San Diego in season opener.
- Scores first NFL rushing touchdown with a 1-yard sneak to give Dallas the season-opening victory over the Chargers on Sept. 9.
- Completes 21 of 26 passes for a career-high 80.8 completion percentage, Sept. 30 at New York Giants.
- Leads Dallas to another come-from-behind victory by directing an 80-yard scoring drive late in the fourth quarter at Tampa Bay.
- Leads the Cowboys' offense on another late game-winning scoring drive at Los Angeles Rams.
- Fashions his first NFL winning streak with consecutive wins over the Rams, Redskins, Saints and Cardinals.
- Dislocates shoulder and is lost for the season after attempting only one pass, Dec. 23 at Philadelphia.

## 1990 [7-9; FOURTH PLACE, NFC EAST]

|  | Att. | Comp. | Yds. | TD | Int. | Long |
|---|---|---|---|---|---|---|
| W- San Diego 9/9 | 29 | 13 | 193 | 1 | 1 | 28t |
| L- N.Y. Giants 9/16 | 18 | 10 | 109 | 0 | 2 | 25 |
| L-@ Washington 9/23 | 43 | 23 | 207 | 0 | 2 | 20 |
| L-@ N.Y. Giants 9/30 | 26 | 21 | 233 | 1 | 1 | 23 |
| W- Tampa Bay 10/7 | 24 | 17 | 173 | 1 | 1 | 30 |
| L-@ Phoenix 10/14 | 25 | 9 | 61 | 0 | 2 | 13 |
| W-@ Tampa Bay 10/21 | 29 | 13 | 159 | 1 | 1 | 28t |
| L- Philadelphia 10/28 | 41 | 22 | 233 | 1 | 1 | 29t |
| L-@ N.Y. Jets 11/4 | 40 | 25 | 249 | 0 | 2 | 51 |
| L- San Francisco 11/11 | 21 | 9 | 96 | 0 | 1 | 26 |
| W-@ L.A. Rams 11/18 | 32 | 17 | 303 | 3 | 1 | 61t |
| W- Washington 11/22 | 31 | 20 | 222 | 1 | 2 | 41 |
| W- New Orleans 12/2 | 21 | 15 | 177 | 1 | 0 | 45 |
| W- Phoenix 12/16 | 18 | 12 | 164 | 1 | 1 | 41 |
| L-@ Philadelphia 12/23 | 1 | 0 | 0 | 0 | 0 | 0 |
| L-@ Atlanta 12/30 | DNP - dislocated shoulder | | | | | |
| **Totals** | **399** | **226** | **2,579** | **11** | **18** | **61t** |

LOUIS DeLUCA

# 1991

- Claims NFC Offensive Player of the Week honors for leading the Cowboys to an upset victory, Sept. 29 over the defending Super Bowl champion New York Giants.
- Records a career-high 31 completions, including 12 straight to end the game during Dallas' 20-17 win over Green Bay, Oct. 6.
- Throws for a season-high 331 yards at Detroit, Oct. 27.
- Posts at least one touchdown pass in four consecutive games during the middle of the season.
- Sprains the lateral collateral ligament in his right knee during the Cowboys' 24-21 win at Washington.
- Earns his first trip to the NFL Pro Bowl.

**1991 [11-5; SECOND PLACE, NFC EAST]**

|  | Att. | Comp. | Yds. | TD | Int. | Long |
|---|---|---|---|---|---|---|
| W-@ Cleveland 9/1 | 37 | 24 | 274 | 2 | 0 | 23 |
| L- Washington 9/9 | 42 | 27 | 242 | 3 | 0 | 29 |
| L- Philadelphia 9/15 | 25 | 11 | 112 | 0 | 3 | 27 |
| W-@ Phoenix 9/22 | 20 | 12 | 150 | 0 | 0 | 26 |
| W- N.Y. Giants 9/29 | 27 | 20 | 277 | 1 | 0 | 38 |
| W-@ Green Bay 10/6 | 41 | 31 | 287 | 1 | 0 | 26 |
| W- Cincinnati 10/13 | 22 | 14 | 276 | 1 | 2 | 61 |
| L-@ Detroit 10/27 | 42 | 28 | 331 | 1 | 2 | 49 |
| W- Phoenix 11/3 | 23 | 17 | 191 | 0 | 2 | 37 |
| L-@ Houston 11/10 | 39 | 24 | 260 | 1 | 0 | 25 |
| L-@ N.Y. Giants 11/17 | 25 | 16 | 150 | 0 | 0 | 22 |
| W-@ Washington 11/24 | 20 | 13 | 204 | 1 | 1 | 39 |
| W- Pittsburgh 11/28 | DNP - sprained knee | | | | | |
| W- New Orleans 12/8 | DNP - sprained knee | | | | | |
| W-@ Philadelphia 12/15 | DNP - sprained knee | | | | | |
| W- Atlanta 12/22 | DNP - sprained knee | | | | | |
| **Totals** | **363** | **237** | **2,754** | **11** | **10** | **61** |

**PLAYOFFS**

|  | Att. | Comp. | Yds. | TD | Int. | Long |
|---|---|---|---|---|---|---|
| W-@ Chicago 12/29 | DNP - sprained knee | | | | | |
| L-@ Detroit 1/5/92 | 16 | 11 | 114 | 0 | 1 | 25 |
| Playoff Totals | 16 | 11 | 114 | 0 | 1 | 25 |

# 1992

- Leads Dallas to an early season victory over the defending Super Bowl champions for the second consecutive season by completing 18 of 31 passes for 216 yards against the Redskins.
- Fashions a streak of five consecutive games in which he throws at least two touchdown passes.
- Completes seven of eight passes for 78 yards during a late touchdown-scoring drive that gives the Cowboys a 31-27 victory Dec. 6 at Denver.
- Completes 13 consecutive passes during an 18-of-21 performance (85.7 percent) during Dallas' 41-17 win at Atlanta.
- Finishes second in the NFC to 49ers quarterback Steve Young and fourth in the NFL in yards passing.
- Throws eight touchdown passes and no interceptions during the Cowboys' three-game run to the Super Bowl championship.
- Earns MVP Award in Super Bowl XXVII after completing 22 of 30 passes for 273 yards and four touchdowns in Dallas' 52-17 romp over Buffalo.

## 1992 [13-3; SUPER BOWL XXVII CHAMPIONS]

| | Att. | Comp. | Yds. | TD | Int. | Long |
|---|---|---|---|---|---|---|
| W- Washington 9/7 | 31 | 18 | 216 | 1 | 2 | 29 |
| W-@ N.Y. Giants 9/13 | 35 | 22 | 238 | 2 | 0 | 27t |
| W- Phoenix 9/20 | 21 | 14 | 263 | 3 | 0 | 87t |
| L-@ Philadelphia 10/5 | 38 | 19 | 256 | 1 | 3 | 59 |
| W- Seattle 10/11 | 23 | 15 | 173 | 0 | 2 | 24 |
| W- Kansas City 10/18 | 29 | 21 | 192 | 1 | 2 | 22 |
| W-@ L.A. Raiders 10/25 | 25 | 16 | 234 | 0 | 0 | 52 |
| W- Philadelphia 11/1 | 33 | 19 | 214 | 2 | 1 | 25 |
| W-@ Detroit 11/8 | 25 | 16 | 214 | 1 | 1 | 57 |
| L- L.A. Rams 11/15 | 37 | 22 | 272 | 0 | 0 | 49 |
| W-@ Phoenix 11/22 | 36 | 25 | 237 | 2 | 1 | 37t |
| W- N.Y. Giants 11/26 | 29 | 19 | 143 | 2 | 1 | 26t |
| W-@ Denver 12/6 | 35 | 25 | 231 | 3 | 0 | 22 |
| L-@ Washington 12/13 | 35 | 23 | 245 | 2 | 1 | 40 |
| W-@ Atlanta 12/21 | 21 | 18 | 239 | 3 | 0 | 37 |
| W- Chicago 12/27 | 20 | 10 | 78 | 0 | 0 | 13 |
| **Totals** | **473** | **302** | **3,445** | **23** | **14** | **87t** |

## PLAYOFFS

| | Att. | Comp. | Yds. | TD | Int. | Long |
|---|---|---|---|---|---|---|
| W- Philadelphia 1/10 | 25 | 15 | 200 | 2 | 0 | 41 |
| W-@ San Francisco 1/17/93 | 34 | 24 | 322 | 2 | 0 | 70 |
| W- Buffalo 1/31/93 | 30 | 22 | 273 | 4 | 0 | 45t |
| **Playoff Totals** | **89** | **61** | **795** | **8** | **0** | **70** |

**TROY AIKMAN**

# 1993

- Fires an 80-yard touchdown pass to Alvin Harper for the team's first score of '93 season during its season-opening loss to Washington.
- Posts a career-high 45 pass attempts during Week 2 loss to Buffalo.
- Completes at least 75 percent of his passes in three consecutive games (Weeks 3-5).
- Earns NFC Offensive Player of the Week honors for an 18-of-23, 317-yard performance vs. Green Bay.
- Wins NFC Offensive Player of the Month for October after leading the Cowboys to four victories in the month.
- Strains left hamstring vs. New York Giants on Nov. 7 and misses the next two games.
- Falls six pass attempts short of Don Meredith's team record of 156 consecutive pass attempts without an interception during Thanksgiving Day game vs. Miami.
- Suffers concussion early in the third quarter of the NFC Championship game after guiding Dallas to a 28-7 lead.
- Claims NFL Alumni Quarterback of the Year Award.

**1993 [12-4; SUPER BOWL XXVIII CHAMPIONS]**

| | Att. | Comp. | Yds. | TD | Int. | Long |
|---|---|---|---|---|---|---|
| L-@ Washington 9/6 | 29 | 17 | 267 | 2 | 0 | 80t |
| L- Buffalo 9/12 | 45 | 28 | 297 | 0 | 2 | 23 |
| W-@ Phoenix 9/19 | 27 | 21 | 281 | 0 | 0 | 44 |
| W- Green Bay 10/3 | 23 | 18 | 317 | 1 | 0 | 66 |
| W-@ Indianapolis 10/10 | 28 | 21 | 245 | 1 | 0 | 30 |
| W- San Francisco 10/17 | 35 | 21 | 243 | 1 | 0 | 36t |
| W-@ Philadelphia 10/31 | 19 | 9 | 96 | 0 | 0 | 21 |
| W- N.Y. Giants 11/7 | 13 | 11 | 162 | 2 | 0 | 50t |
| W- Phoenix 11/14 | DNP - strained hamstring | | | | | |
| L-@ Atlanta 11/21 | DNP - strained hamstring | | | | | |
| L- Miami 11/25 | 43 | 28 | 181 | 1 | 1 | 19 |
| W- Philadelphia 12/6 | 24 | 17 | 178 | 1 | 0 | 21 |
| W-@ Minnesota 12/12 | 29 | 19 | 208 | 1 | 0 | 37 |
| W-@ N.Y. Jets 12/18 | 27 | 21 | 252 | 2 | 3 | 42t |
| W- Washington 12/26 | 20 | 16 | 193 | 2 | 0 | 30 |
| W-@ N.Y. Giants 1/2/94 | 30 | 24 | 180 | 1 | 0 | 22 |
| **Totals** | **392** | **271** | **3,100** | **15** | **6** | **80t** |

**PLAYOFFS**

| | Att. | Comp. | Yds. | TD | Int. | Long |
|---|---|---|---|---|---|---|
| W- Green Bay 1/16/94 | 37 | 28 | 302 | 3 | 2 | 27 |
| W- San Francisco 1/23/94 | 18 | 14 | 177 | 2 | 0 | 28 |
| W- Buffalo 1/30/94 | 27 | 19 | 207 | 0 | 1 | 35 |
| **Playoff Totals** | **82** | **61** | **686** | **5** | **3** | **35** |

TROY AIKMAN

# 1994

- Earns NFC Offensive Player of the Week Award following a 16-of-22, 231-yard, two-touchdown performance against Arizona.
- Breaks club record of 12 consecutive games with a touchdown pass by connecting with Alvin Harper on a 16-yard toss against Philadelphia, Oct. 16.
- Suffers a concussion on a hit by Arizona's Wilbur Marshall. Just a few plays later, Aikman hits Harper with a 15-yard TD pass before leaving the game for good.
- Throws for 339 yards, including a 90-yard pass to Harper, during the team's loss to San Francisco, Nov. 13.
- Sprains medial collateral ligament in left knee in the second quarter of Dallas' win over Washington and misses the next two games.
- Sets an NFL postseason record with a 94-yard TD pass to Harper during the Cowboys' 35-9 romp over Green Bay in the NFC divisional playoff game.
- Establishes career highs with 380 yards passing and 53 attempts during NFC Championship game loss to the 49ers.
- Participates in his fourth consecutive Pro Bowl.

**1994 [12-4; NFC EAST CHAMPIONS]**

|  | Att. | Comp. | Yds. | TD | Int. | Long |
|---|---|---|---|---|---|---|
| W-@ Pittsburgh 9/4 | 32 | 21 | 245 | 1 | 1 | 38 |
| W- Houston 9/11 | 25 | 14 | 228 | 1 | 1 | 53t |
| L- Detroit 9/19 | 39 | 26 | 220 | 1 | 0 | 20 |
| W-@ Washington 10/2 | 28 | 20 | 181 | 1 | 1 | 46 |
| W- Arizona 10/9 | 22 | 16 | 231 | 2 | 0 | 42 |
| W- Philadelphia 10/16 | 23 | 12 | 156 | 2 | 1 | 18 |
| W-@ Arizona 10/23 | 5 | 3 | 51 | 1 | 0 | 28 |
| W-@ Cincinnati 10/30 | 33 | 20 | 272 | 2 | 1 | 46 |
| W- N.Y. Giants 11/7 | 24 | 19 | 241 | 1 | 0 | 36 |
| L-@ San Francisco 11/13 | 42 | 23 | 339 | 0 | 3 | 90 |
| W- Washington 11/20 | 13 | 8 | 87 | 0 | 0 | 18 |
| W- Green Bay 11/24 | DNP - sprained knee | | | | | |
| W-@ Philadelphia 12/4 | DNP - sprained knee | | | | | |
| L- Cleveland 12/10 | 36 | 21 | 188 | 1 | 2 | 18 |
| W-@ New Orleans 12/19 | 28 | 21 | 175 | 0 | 2 | 22 |
| L-@ N.Y. Giants 12/24 | 11 | 9 | 62 | 0 | 0 | 18 |
| **Totals** | **361** | **233** | **2,676** | **13** | **12** | **90** |

**PLAYOFFS**

|  | Att. | Comp. | Yds. | TD | Int. | Long |
|---|---|---|---|---|---|---|
| W- Green Bay 1/8/95 | 30 | 23 | 337 | 2 | 1 | 94t |
| L-@ San Francisco 1/15/95 | 53 | 30 | 380 | 2 | 3 | 44t |
| Playoff Totals | 83 | 53 | 717 | 4 | 4 | 94t |

**TROY AIKMAN**

# 1995

- Throws three TD passes in Dallas' 31-21 triumph over the Broncos, Sept. 10.
- Completes nine of 11 passes in the fourth quarter and overtime of the next week's 23-17 win at Minnesota.
- Leaves game after straining his left calf muscle on the sixth play of Dallas' 27-23 loss at Washington, Oct. 1.
- Returns from the injury the next week and completes 24 of 31 passes for 316 yards and two touchdowns in leading the Cowboys to a 34-24 victory over the Packers, Oct. 8.
- Bruises knee and is forced out early in the Cowboys' 38-20 loss to San Francisco, Nov. 12.
- Leads Dallas to yet another Super Bowl title by completing more than 66 percent of his passes during the team's postseason run.
- Plays in team-record fifth consecutive Pro Bowl.

**1995 [12-4; SUPER BOWL XXX CHAMPIONS]**

|  | Att. | Comp. | Yds. | TD | Int. | Long |
|---|---|---|---|---|---|---|
| W-@ N.Y. Giants 9/4 | 20 | 15 | 228 | 1 | 0 | 43 |
| W- Denver 9/10 | 31 | 18 | 196 | 2 | 1 | 29 |
| W-@ Minnesota 9/17 | 38 | 24 | 246 | 1 | 0 | 26 |
| W- Arizona 9/24 | 30 | 19 | 251 | 1 | 0 | 50 |
| L-@ Washington 10/1 | 3 | 2 | 30 | 0 | 0 | 23 |
| W- Green Bay 10/8 | 31 | 24 | 316 | 2 | 0 | 48t |
| W-@ San Diego 10/15 | 30 | 21 | 222 | 0 | 0 | 30 |
| W-@ Atlanta 10/29 | 25 | 19 | 198 | 2 | 1 | 43t |
| W- Philadelphia 11/6 | 24 | 17 | 202 | 1 | 1 | 38 |
| L- San Francisco 11/12 | 6 | 4 | 29 | 0 | 1 | 10 |
| W-@ Oakland 11/19 | 24 | 19 | 227 | 1 | 0 | 36 |
| W- Kansas City 11/23 | 29 | 21 | 192 | 2 | 0 | 33t |
| L- Washington 12/3 | 47 | 29 | 285 | 1 | 1 | 23 |
| L-@ Philadelphia 12/10 | 28 | 11 | 110 | 0 | 0 | 19 |
| W- N.Y. Giants 12/17 | 34 | 16 | 222 | 0 | 1 | 40 |
| W-@ Arizona 12/24 | 32 | 21 | 350 | 2 | 1 | 48t |
| **Totals** | **432** | **280** | **3,304** | **16** | **7** | **50** |

**PLAYOFFS**

|  | Att. | Comp. | Yds. | TD | Int. | Long |
|---|---|---|---|---|---|---|
| W- Philadelphia 1/7/96 | 24 | 17 | 253 | 1 | 1 | 37 |
| W- Green Bay 1/14/96 | 33 | 21 | 255 | 2 | 0 | 36 |
| W- Pittsburgh 1/28/96 | 23 | 15 | 209 | 1 | 0 | 47 |
| **Playoff Totals** | **80** | **53** | **717** | **4** | **1** | **47** |

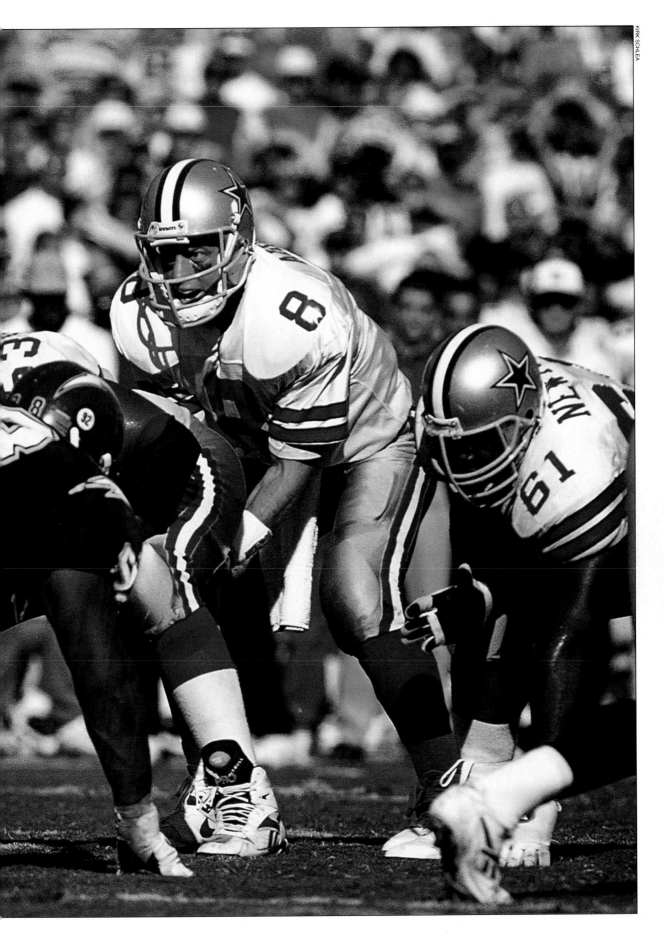

TROY AIKMAN

By Dave Spadaro

# He has won three of the last four Super Bowls.

**He has been tagged as one of the game's most accurate passers.**

He's just 29 years old.

**What's left for Troy Aikman to accomplish when he's already . . .**

# been there, done that.

**n**o, Troy Aikman does not have a halo following his every step. He cannot walk on water. Although, when he tries he doesn't get very wet.

And if it seems he leads a charmed and blessed life, well, understand he's worked hard to be so great. If it seems like Aikman is a dream, rub your eyes and, like he says, "Get real."

He's not just another square jaw and a pretty face. He's the product of polishing what is, quite frankly, an awesome package.

In his seven seasons with the Dallas Cowboys, Aikman has reached the top and, most impressively, stayed there. He's won three Super Bowls, compiling a 10-1 postseason record as a starter. To say the least, Aikman has fulfilled his prophecy "to have some success in football," which was bestowed upon him during his senior prom at Henryetta (Okla.) High School.

Aikman has it all — acclaim as one of the game's best, a multimillion-dollar contract that runs through the 2000 season, adoration from legions of Cowboys fans from sea to shining sea and commercial endorsements worth even more.

He's earned the envy of every teammate and the respect of every opponent.

"I look at my team and what we need to get better, to win the Super Bowl, and then I look at the Cowboys," says Philadelphia Eagles head coach Ray Rhodes. "I get to the quarterback position and I see Troy Aikman and I think, 'Man, how many more years is he going to play?' Him being there makes my job a whole lot harder.

"I've got to be honest," Rhodes continues. "As long as the Cowboys have Troy Aikman, it's going to be real hard for the Eagles to beat them. He's the guy who makes that team go. He's got everything from the standpoint of being a quarterback. Every coach wishes he had Troy. I just wish he'd hurry up and get tired of the game."

That isn't likely to happen, at least not anytime soon. Aikman, who holds or has tied more than 30 Cowboys records, is, theoretically, entering the prime of his career.

Is there any reason to think Dallas won't win a Super Bowl or two or three between now and 2000? No, not with the core group of Aikman, running back Emmitt Smith and wide

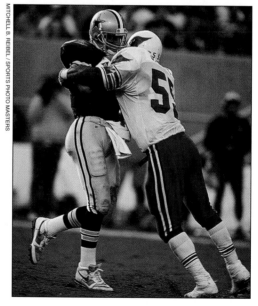

Only the threat of being pounded into a premature retirement is likely to prevent Troy from polishing his already glossy NFL resume.

receiver Michael Irvin intact.

And with owner Jerry Jones committed to the cause, the sky is the limit for the Cowboys, and Aikman. That's certainly the feeling around the Cowboys, who are under the gun each season. A good season is a win in the Super Bowl. Anything less is considered a bad season.

In fact, during the course of the 1995 regular season, red flags were sent up when word spread that Aikman was considering an early

**TROY AIKMAN**

**TROY AIKMAN**

As long as Aikman's standing tall in the pocket and barking signals for the Cowboys, the sky's the limit on what else he can accomplish with Dallas' franchise in the '90s.

retirement, citing health concerns and a lack of enjoyment in the game.

Aikman laid those fears to rest by charging down the homestretch and through the playoffs with nearly pinpoint-perfect performances and a sigh of relief at season's end.

"I enjoy the winning aspect of the game and I enjoy the challenge of the game," he says. "I'm not going anywhere. I'm going to stay here and keep us winning.

"We've got a lot more we can accomplish."

They do? Three Super Bowls in four seasons isn't enough? Soon Aikman and Jones will have their own cable station hawking pizzas, jerseys, autographs, framed kisses.

Sound ridiculous? Maybe. But as long as No. 8 stays on the field, there's very little he and the Cowboys can't do.

"With Troy, we've always got the foundation," says Smith, the All-World back. "It all starts with the quarterback, and we've got a great one. We have confidence in him. I don't see why we can't keep winning as long as we stay healthy."

The nature of Aikman's game is to win — and win big. With his three Super victories, he's narrowing the gap on Terry Bradshaw and Joe Montana, each of whom has won four Super Bowls and lost none. Aikman should surpass their record by, say, 1999.

"Troy is playing at a very high level right now," says Jones, the owner who deserves credit for keeping the Dallas dynasty intact. "I think he's got better football in him. I think he's a special quarterback with a drive that is unsurpassed. Troy doesn't accept losing. He won't. He is everything you look for in a quarterback, and I don't see any signs he's slowing down."

Aikman already holds the Cowboys' top quarterback rating at 83.5, which is also seventh-best in NFL history. He's an amazing 70-39 in 109 career starts. And when you take into account his 1-14 record in his first 15 starts, you see how remarkable he's been since his early days.

Plus, Aikman boasts a career completion percentage of 62.8 percent, third-best in NFL history behind just Steve Young and Montana. Since 1991, he has completed 60 percent of his passes in 68 of 84 games and has thrown a touchdown pass in 38 of his last 49 games.

"That stuff, I don't care about it," he says. "All that's important to me is winning. That makes me happy."

No wonder, then, that Aikman has an ear-to-ear grin plastered on his face. Get used to the look. The Best of Troy Aikman lies ahead. The Quarterback of the '90s is just coming into his own, guns blazing. •

*Dave Spadaro covers the NFL for* Eagles Digest.

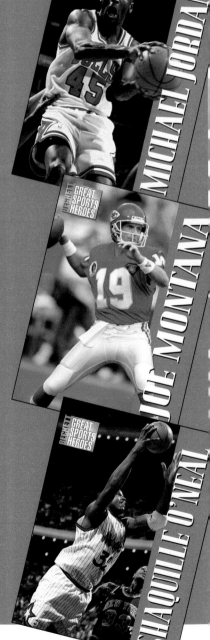